Wiccan Spirituality

A system of Wiccan spirituality and magic for the 21st century

Kevin Saunders

Green Magic

This edition is published by
Green Magic
BCM Inspire
London WC1N 3XX

Typeset by Academic + Technical, Bristol
Printed and bound by Antony Rowe Ltd, Chippenham

Cover design by Chris Render

Cover artwork by Trystan Mitchell © 2002

ISBN 0 9536631 6 7

GREEN MAGIC

ABOUT THE AUTHOR

Kevin Saunders was born in 1960 in Harrow, Middlesex, north west of London, England. He went to Stag Lane Junior School and Downer Grammar, before leaving to work for the local council. Having soon become bored with this he left to tour with bands around Europe and the United States for a number of years before settling for marriage to a farmer's daughter and moving to Saffron Walden in Essex.

He was active in many animal rights and ecological campaigns and active politically through the Green Party. As Chairman of the Saffron Walden Green Party he stood in District and County Council elections before moving to start up his own business in Cornwall selling organic and vegetarian wholefoods. Whilst in Cornwall he worked with the League Against Cruel Sports as regional representative and stood for Parliament against Sebastian Coe for the Green Party.

After six years of running his own business he moved into the professional public relations field by first becoming Senior Press Officer for the League Against Cruel Sports in London and represented them on numerous TV and radio programmes and debates all over the country. He also helped found an environmental think-tank called the Campaign for Political Ecology for which he worked on its National Executive Committee for a short time. He then went on to work as Chief Press Officer for the Green Party (UK) and helped get two MEPs elected to the European Parliament.

For many years, whilst working for many environmental campaigns, he considered himself an atheist. He began to develop his spiritual aspects early in his thirties, though at the time unable to put a label on his own beliefs that were centred on environmentalism, animal rights, feminism and socially responsible politics. He eventually discovered paganism and witchcraft, an event that was to open his eyes wide and change his life. He studied and practised hard and worked his way through the degree system of Wicca to become a High Priest of his craft.

He is now living with his partner Tania in Glastonbury, which he considers has been a spiritual finishing school for many throughout the ages. He is working as a tutor for the Isle of Avalon Foundation and an environmental charity based in Bristol.

DEDICATION

To Morgana, who helped me reach the darkest of places,
From where I learnt to experience the Light

WITH SPECIAL THANKS TO...

To my mother, whose love is unconditional, non-judgemental and
supportive.
To Lightgift, whose gift of light shines through the darkest of places,
her tremendous support for which my deep gratitude is hardly adequate.
To Seaspirit, for the love, inspiration and constant encouragement.
To Misstyke, for making me laugh and keeping my feet on the ground
(no you can't use a pink plastic wand with flashing lights on the top!)
To my sister, for the sanctuary when I most needed it.
To Em, who taught me so much about trees, herbs and myself.
To Shely, for that fateful day when she asked 'do you know anything
about magic?'

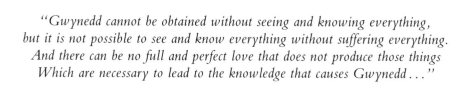

*"Gwynedd cannot be obtained without seeing and knowing everything,
but it is not possible to see and know everything without suffering everything.
And there can be no full and perfect love that does not produce those things
Which are necessary to lead to the knowledge that causes Gwynedd..."*

CONTENTS

1

INTRODUCTION

The rituals of Gardnerian Wicca (and the various forms of Wicca that developed from it) have opened up a whole new system of spirituality for many. For those looking for something with a greater depth to it than Christianity, something that is closer to the natural ways we are drawn to, and a system that encourages the individual to be empowered through self development and by finding the divine within, looking to the past has allowed us to find a system that is much more suitable to the fill in the gaps left by a modern life style.

Gardnerian Wicca certainly more than inspired me to start with. This book is based on what I have discovered through my study of Wicca, Celtic Witchcraft and Druidism, as well as the many magical traditions going back through to their roots in ancient Greece, Persia and Egypt.

This book represents a revision of *Witchcraft for the 21st Century* that I have most definitely developed, quite unashamedly in my own style. I have no intention of suggesting that my way is any better than that of any other way. I simply offer it because I have found it to work for me where other systems failed. If this works for you then that is wonderful. If this book inspires you to develop your own system that works even better for you, than that is wonderful too. This work is entirely personal and needs to be for reasons that I hope will become clear as you study this book. In places I include my feelings on the state-controlled church, which may contain a certain element of cynicism. That is because my early years were spent being introduced to the Church of England and having rejected its dogma, and what I see as its hypocrisy, I ended up rejecting all forms of spirituality for many years, preferring to consider myself an atheist. Basically I chucked out the baby with the bath water. In many ways this was a great shame, though I suppose I would never have got to where I am without it, so I should be grateful. In retrospect I realise that I have been living and working as a pagan for most of my life; I just hadn't appreciated that my beliefs had a sound spiritual basis that had a readily available label.

1

My advice to anyone seeking any form of spiritual path is that you should accept nothing that doesn't feel right to you. Following your own intuition and ensuring the symbolism you discover links firmly with your own inner or higher self is essential if you are to walk the mystical spiral path inwards and successfully find your way out.

Wicca was the catalyst that made me realise there was a spiritual system that fits in with the way I feel we should relate to everything around us. It is a system that enabled me to discover the amazing energies that can be tapped into and utilised. I am a pagan witch for sure – one that has been initiated to the third degree and allows me the right to use what I fear is a rather pretentious sounding title of 'High Priest' – but my path has led me to develop my own system. I have continued to call it Wicca, for it follows the pattern of understanding and working that has been laid down by those who have gone before me.

One cannot learn witchcraft straight from a book any more than one can play a piece of classical music by having cast ones eyes over the sheet music. Wicca is not a path for a spectator, but for a participator. Ceremonies mean little if the understanding is something which is taught by others and does not resonate with oneself. The belief and true understanding has to come from one's higher self; the deities we associate with and the way we see the Divine Source (and the name we give it if indeed we choose to give it a name) has to come from within. It has to really mean something to us, and what makes us an individual, a responsible member of the community, as well as a guardian of the physical plane. What makes us all different are things such as our upbringing, our culture, our experiences in this life and others, the environment in which we live, and the soul group to which we belong. To produce a system that can be standardised is simply not going to work. For that reason, whilst I have presented here what works for me, I have done my best to encourage those reading it to question what I have written, question what they believe, and transfer their own correspondences for mine whenever anything doesn't feel right – or indeed reject the whole thing if it all feels so uncomfortable.

What I have tried to do throughout this book is to present a form of Wicca that brings the understanding of the Craft into the present millennium. I have presented it as a form of witchcraft that utilises the wisdom of the old religion, with what has been learnt from other esoteric disciplines, with a relevance to our future in the 21st Century and the challenges it brings. I have presented a version of the some of the rituals that fit with those used in the past, but with some of the 'Olde English' updated so that it is easier to understand, appreciate, and in my view, flows better. In the process of doing this I have removed what I consider to be some of the inconsistencies that are apparent to

2

me from the original Gardnerian and Alexandrian texts. I have done this without taking away any of the essential elements contained in the original. Bear in mind, however, that you should always feel free and prepared to use your own form of words. The strongest form of ritual is one that you have put energy into and devised yourself – a matter that has always been consistent with the teachings of Wicca from its outset.

As we enter the new millennium we face many challenges. We need to learn to live together in peace and harmony and solve conflicts without resorting to murder, terrorism and war. We need to learn to live within the means provided by our environment and to learn respect for one another and for our Mother Earth. She has provided us with a beauty and bounty that we should cherish and nurture as her caring loving children and join with our higher selves to bring the worlds of spirit and form closer so that we may one day all live life for the love of itself and to all that it is connected.

Good luck on your path and Blessed Be.

2

A BRIEF HISTORY OF PAGANISM AND WITCHCRAFT

Many of those who practise witchcraft today go to extraordinary lengths in trying to prove that their version of the Craft can trace its origins back to practices of pagans and/or esoteric traditions that go back many thousands of years. I consider many of the claims that have been made to be highly speculative, impossible to prove, and in many if not most cases, highly unlikely. Whilst I appreciate and have no reason to doubt that some people possess knowledge and abilities that have been either handed down or inherited through several generations, the obsession with proving a link to a deep ancestry is unnecessary. Whilst a brief look at the history of paganism and witchcraft is useful and interesting, we must remember that what is important is how we apply its uses to today and the future. Certainly the claims that modern Wicca can trace its roots through the ages when it is almost certainly a system that has been constructed from a great many esoteric paths including the knowledge of the traditional village wise-women, skilled in the use of herbs and folk magic, and the more formal rituals of mystical christianity, druidry and freemasonry is both spurious and absurd even if there are clearly many common roots. The anthropological history is a matter of great interest for historians to unravel, not for those wishing to step onto the path in the 21st Century.

Nature worship can be traced back to the very earliest of prehistoric human tribes. It is understandable how early humankind, as hunter-gathers, began to create an understanding of the divine based on the animals that they relied upon as food such as the stag. Later as agriculture and husbandry began to develop, along with the intricacy of the human mind and civilisation, an understanding of nature, the changing seasons and the power of, and relationship to, the earth, sun and moon, created a more elaborate set of deities to hold in awe and wonder. The worship of and respect for nature's aspects and energies enabled our ancestors to respect the environment in a way that would certainly not allow the modern ecological disasters that have been caused by our modern blinkered faith in segregated science. It appears that our ancestors were well aware of the abundant natural energies and worked with and accepted them in ways that have largely been forgotten, and yet can be rediscovered.

There is evidence that the earliest agricultural civilisations of the eastern Mediterranean and Middle East, as well as other apparently unconnected civilisations across the globe, worshipped both a Goddess and a God, or more accurately saw the divine source of all manifest itself in what could be more easily digested as aspects of various goddesses and gods. It is assumed by many historians (largely male historians) that before male-dominated society started to gradually push out a true feminine aspect of divinity that the civilisations worshipping goddesses were female-dominated, that they were matriarchal rather than patriarchal. There is, however, evidence that these civilisations were *not* dominated by either sex. It does not necessarily follow that one gender dominating the other is the only option, or by any means the most ideal. Whist the Goddesses were of prime importance, leading to the prevalence of feminine values (nurturing, caring, sharing, etc) within those societies, they also worshipped a God, or masculine, values as well. They found a delicate balance between masculine and feminine that worked as a partnership model rather than a dominator model.

It would appear that the last civilisation to survive the gradual onslaught of the Piscean influenced male-dominated societies (with all the unbalanced aggression and selfishness that came with it) was Crete. The ancient Cretans had no need to build their towns and villages in fortified positions. Their worship of the Goddess and God produced a society that had little need of weapons of destruction, was clearly devoid of hierarchy, shared the wealth relatively equally among all its inhabitants and lived in peace for a longer period than probably any other society throughout history.[1]

Modern society would do very well to note the effect of this partnership model of society that worshipped the divine in both its feminine and masculine aspects. Such a model should certainly encourage those amongst our peers who would like to see a society based more on equality, ecological prudence and peace. I do fear, however, that some amongst the new age neo-pagans who want to replace worship of a male god with the female goddess have severely missed the point. The secret is partnership and balance between male and female rather than dominance of one over the other, and this relationship needs to prevail

---

[1] See *The Chalice and the Blade* by Riane Eisler.

through religion, politics and all the sciences. We are sadly a long way from achieving such a goal. The male-dominance within modern society is resisting strongly any move to such reforms and will resist even more strongly as they become more and more prevalent, despite the obvious benefits for society as a whole. On the other hand, those who are pushing for such reforms will do well to address the way they present themselves – a matter which I personally find is often very disappointing and far from progressive.

What we know of the societies worshipping the Goddess and God in balance and partnership can only be found through anthropological study of the evidence in ancient ruins. These civilisations began to be destroyed by barbarian invasions around 4300 BCE with Crete finally falling around 3,000 years ago. Since then it would appear that no such partnership model of society has existed and male dominance has ruled and gained strength to the present time. Rather than disappearing altogether, the pagan beliefs became modified. The attributes of various goddess images began to take on warrior or hunting (i.e. masculine) elements. Goddess elements did survive, however, and remained vital aspects of pagan belief and worship even though the political leaders of the tribes tended to be male and the God aspects stood above rather than beside the Goddess.

As the pagan mythology of ancient civilisations became dominated by men, it survived and spread across from Egypt, Mesopotamia and Greece to western and northern Europe arriving in Britain and Ireland at a very early date. As tribes moved and intermingled with others, the mythology that moved with it combined and superimposed upon that which already existed. By the time the Celts arrived in Britain, there was already a flourishing pagan form of worship among the natives based on a horned god.

Those pagan belief systems appear to have a Solar orientated focus. Places of worship, such as Stonehenge, were aligned to the Sun. The Celts brought with them the ancient nature-based mythology which had gradually changed and developed into a variety of anthropomorphic guises. A theme that remained central to all Celtic belief systems was our connection to spirits, gods and elementals in 'the Otherworld' or another dimension. It is impossible to tell to what degree this contact was prevalent, at least among the ordinary members of each tribe, but the historical records make it quite clear that the belief in birth, death and rebirth, whether in this dimension or another, were very strong. The teachings of the spiritual leaders of the times certainly involved the development of 'second sight' that is evident throughout the mythological texts that have survived. The spiritual leaders were in effect in control even of the political leaders of the times. Kings were held responsible for the success of the tribe, the fertility of the land and were even, it seems, subject to sacrifice in order to maintain that success.

It is difficult to identify those who practised witchcraft, as we know it today, in the early years. The spiritual leaders were more likely druids who worked primarily with the Sun and occult work seems to have been more shamanic in design than anything else. The knowledge was passed down through the generations through analogies rather than being written down in a straight forward fashion as is often the case throughout religious history. There were almost certainly those amongst the tribes who developed knowledge of herbs, for medicinal purposes, and those herbs would also have been used by shamans to help reach an intoxicated trance state.

During the years of the Roman Empire a more politically imposed form of paganism was superimposed once again on top of the native belief systems. As the Romans' military might spread throughout Europe, new Gods and Goddesses were introduced that had similar attributes to those they replaced. These Roman deities, themselves drawn largely from Greek and Persian systems which had already been drawn and adapted from Egyptian and Sumerian systems, were constantly changing and were based on anthropomorphic representations totally alien to the Celtic concept.

During this period a grouping known as the Gnostics broke away from the eastern Mediterranean system of Judaism, which itself (though male-dominated) was developing its own mystic system, and started revising and combining the mythology of the Greeks, Egyptians and Persians into a system that became Christianity. The mythology of Osirus, Dionysus and Mithras became combined with that of Judaism putting a new character in the place of previous primary god figures. Whether or not there was a Jesus figure in real life is irrelevant. The fact that most of the stories that involved him in the original Gnostic texts can be found in similar form amongst mythological teachings of previous pagan deities is inescapable.[2]

Personally I believe that Jesus was a real person. Most probably a skilled magician and healer trained by the Essenes and who taught that the Goddess and God could be found within. It is equally possible that Celtic druids, or Platonistic adepts, were involved in his teaching, whether in the eastern Mediterranean or in Britain (there were strong trading links with Cornwall and the South West of England – there is much speculation that Joseph of Arimathea, Jesus's uncle, was such a trader and came to Britain possibly with the young Jesus in tow). He may well have been a talented student who soon became thoroughly

---

[2] *The Jesus Mysteries – Was Jesus a Pagan God?*

adept and able to perform 'miraculous' healing to those who came to him by utilising the energies modern healers of many traditions tap in to. He would also have been seen as a threat to the Jews which by his time would not have tolerated the idea of women being on an equal footing with men, or that each sexual gender has access to the divine within. He would also have been a threat to the Romans for much the same reason. At the time, the official state religion of the Romans would have been Mithras which, although definitively pagan, was also very much a male dominated path.

I very much doubt that Jesus would have claimed to be '*the* son of God', though he may well have said that he was '*a* son of God' − a vital difference. I find it doubtful that Jesus would have wanted to see a Church built around his name, and would almost certainly have been horrified to see that Church develop into a system that insisted that the divine could only be found through the state controlled religion and the punishment for not worshipping through the Church's heirarchy, and in compliance to its considerable dogma, was damnation in hell and in some cases death.

Early Gnostic Christianity gradually became popular. As with the pagan teachings on which it was based it taught that the divine spirit resides within each of us. As such there was no need to worship the many faces of deity imposed on civilisation by the ruling Romans, and by doing so threatened the political stability through such anarchic individualistic beliefs. After a brief flirt with Christianity and a move back to Mithras, the Romans eventually decided that Christianity would become the official religion throughout its Empire. It was a case of if you can't beat them, join them. However, having taken control of Christianity, the Roman church took the Gnostic texts on which their form of pagan-inspired Christianity was based and rewrote them considerably, destroying a great deal in order that religious belief was not a matter of individuality but the way to the divine could only be found through a centrally-organised Church that was essentially state-controlled. To make matters worse, the Bible, despite its many and blatant self-contradictions that survive to this day, was expected to be taken as a literal historical account rather than a set of allegorical inner mystery teachings.

By the time Jesus appeared at the start of the male-dominated Age of Pisces, many hermetic paths had been developed in Egypt, Persia, Greece, Rome, Britain and Ireland, Scandinavia and throughout the rest of the world. Most of these were what we would recognise as pagan in its modern sense. The Goddess image had survived in each, though subtly and gradually the God aspects had become superior. The associated correspondences with the Goddess, the feminine, had themselves been given masculine associations on top of their original. For some those aspects have been carried through to paganism today and have been picked up by some following a feminist path. Some people who claim to be 'into' a warrior goddess because as a woman it gives them strength and inspiration to tackle the male dominated business world of the 21st century are in fact tapping into male correspondences. However, if that helps bring the balance necessary for that person to find the balance they need to develop then I see no great harm in it other than being ignorant of the true origins or elemental reality. To me it is about finding balance between the feminine and masculine aspects that reside within each of us and recognising that as a fact rather than denying it.

By the fourth century of the current era, the Roman Church had completely re-written and transformed the figure of Jesus and the pagan-inspired stories of him found in the Gnostic texts. The New Testament gradually got whittled down to such a degree that the implicit inner teachings were watered down, and became all but lost, and the rest became to be expected to be read as a literal account of Jesus's life. The pagan festivals were transformed into Christian festivals in order to make them more acceptable to the populace on which Christianity was to be imposed. For instance; Christmas[3] was positioned at Yule (the birth of the Sun/Son); Ostara became Easter (the resurrection or spring); Samhain or Halloween became All Saints Day; etc.

Christianity gradually developed into a dualistic system involving heaven and hell. If one didn't worship God through the Church then one would be condemned to eternal misery in a Hell ruled by the Devil – or Satan – a figure introduced to Christianity in the 14th Century. Rather than worshipping a Goddess figure – that of a pregnant woman, or a symbol of life – Christians worshipped a man on a cross – a symbol of death and the fear of what would happen after death.

The introduction of Christianity started at an early date. It is believed that Jesus's Uncle, Joseph of Aramathea, came to the South West of England on a trading boat and introduced the first Christian mission at Glastonbury – a site that has always been a site steeped in pagan mythology. However, paganism was not so easily overcome. In Britain at least, the new religion mingled quite easily with traditional Celtic beliefs as they were presented in a way that was entirely familiar. The Christianised Celtic Church gradually took over the sites of power used by the Druids by building churches on them and many of the pagan deities were transformed into saints. The Celtic Church withstood

---

[3] December 25th was originally celebrated as the birth of Mithras, moved from January 6th, the birth of Osirus, which by way of compromise became the 'twelfth night'.

pressure from its Roman parentage for many years, working much more in the pagan forms of worship than Rome would eventually tolerate.

However, paganism in its natural form survived alongside the new religion, especially in the further reaches of the community, but also amongst the sovereignty who remained stubbornly pagan through many centuries. Kings of England were encouraged by the Church of Rome to turn to Christianity for the sake of their trading situation with the rest of Europe, though this was a long process. It was not until King William Rufus was sacrificed (though some say he was killed by accident) in the New Forest by way of an arrow that the last openly pagan King was replaced on the throne. Among the peasantry, paganism lasted much longer. Having lost the leadership of the Druids in their formal role, witchcraft probably survived amongst the villages in a style more akin to that which we know it today, though gradually being pushed underground as the State began to get tough in wiping out the 'old ways'. For several hundred years, books were burnt and people were either hung or burnt as witches throughout Europe in an attempt to wipe the Old Religion off the face of the globe in a holocaust possibly matching that faced by the Jews of the Second World War (estimates of the numbers killed vary enormously). Accusing a hated neighbour (more often than not a female) of being a witch was to condemn her to the inquisition that rarely seemed to take no for an answer. It is likely that many of those who were tortured, made to confess and subsequently killed were not actually practising witchcraft at all. The unreasonable way that people were treated is typified by the Salem witch trials in the USA which led to many people being accused of witchcraft and several hanged. After an epidemic that caused many to experience violent fits and hallucinations (most likely caused by a toxic fungus on the crops). The medics of the time could find no cause other than the 'supernatural' and blamed witchcraft. Those accused were given the choice to confess or hang – no option to prove their inno- cence – and many therefore chose to be hanged.

Paganism, rather than being dualistic (as Christianity is today), is both monotheistic and polytheistic. Pagans tend to recognise one divine (mono- theistic) source from which there are seen many aspects that can take either feminine (goddess) or masculine (god) virtues of many hues (polytheistic). Pagans believe that we are all capable of good and 'evil' and are responsible to the divine through oneself for the choices one makes in this. Pagans therefore do not believe in the duality of Heaven and Hell, or God and Satan or live in fear of death and eternal condemnation if one puts a foot wrong though tend to recognise and accept the responsibility to put things right if they do wrong. They do not have the option of blaming bad deeds on the work of 'the Devil' taking the more difficult option of accepting that we are each far from perfect, though striving to improve at every step.

Pagans see the divine manifest in nature. We see the divine alive in the trees, in the mountains, in the earth, the moon and the sun, in everything throughout the cosmos. We see the goddesses and gods as part of nature that is sometimes benevolent and sometimes harsh and cruel. We see ourselves as intimately connected to nature, as part of nature, and therefore as part of the divine. Nature teaches us that we live in a world that is a constant cycle of birth, death and rebirth, and understand that our life follows this cycle just as everything around us does. In seeing the environment within which we live as part of the divine that includes ourselves, we learn to live our lives by the laws of nature and to respect the cycles of life, death and rebirth that are inescapable and inevitable. We learn that we can contact and work with the energies that nature provides in us and around us for our own benefit, for the benefit of those around us, and the benefit of the environment in which we live as each is equally part of the divine and as such deserves respect. Pagans understand that death is not just an ending, but a new beginning, just as it is in the cycle of the seasons, and that our spirit continues to live and grow as our ever expanding stockpile of experiences allow us the understanding of all that is valuable to us as an intimate and inseparable part of the whole.

3

PAGANISM AND WITCHCRAFT TODAY

Earth, Gaia, our Mother, our home. One planet among a host of planets, moons, asteroids and comets in a solar system which is but one of millions within a galaxy that itself is but one of an infinite number of galaxies.

Earth is essentially a living organism in Her own right. Just as in our living bodies, She has a warm heart, a nervous system, energy channels and an ever changing outer surface that lives and breathes. It is from Her thin outer surface that we interact with Her and other living plants, creatures and elements like individual cells each with an inter-dependent role to play. Our physical bodies are born, and just as with all other organisms our physical bodies eventually die and return to the Earth to perpetuate a never ending cycle.

In recent years we have come to abuse the space we live in. We exploit the resources that are available to us in order to enrich ourselves materially in a desperate search for satisfaction, for happiness and for spiritual freedom. In this vain and hopeless search we desecrate that which we need for our very survival and cause pain, destruction and suffering at every turn. Environmentalists cry out 'Save the Planet!' and yet our benevolent Mother Earth is not under threat. Nature will purge itself of that which causes it damage and repair the Earth in time, just as our own individual bodies have ways of purging themselves of damaging organisms. The human race may well threaten its own survival – the planet itself will recover eventually. Our faith in modern science provides an excuse for inaction as we have, throughout the past two thousand years of the Piscean Age, positioned ourselves above Nature, yet one look at the devastation that can be caused by a hurricane, or a depleted ozone layer, or a raging volcano should be enough to remind us of the respect we should have, if not for the Earth, then for our very own survival.

Early human communities lived closely alongside Nature. Throughout the Bronze and Iron Ages a respectful reverence for what many now call Gaia was necessary for survival. The more advanced

12

pagan civilisations, in many ways more advanced than ours today, did not separate science from spirituality. They did not see Nature as an adversary, but as a potentially benevolent partner to be respected. The early philosophers, scientists and mathematicians were at the same time the spiritual leaders. There was no compartmentalisation of disciplines; they worked holistically and understood the limits within which they had to work. They understood that the Earth was a sphere, that the Sun was at the centre of the solar system – they even managed to work out the very size of the planet – and yet centuries later, after we entered the Age of Pisces, those connections were lost, the learning rejected. The dogma introduced by the Roman Church demanded obedient subservience more for the sake of political control than spirituality. It also demanded that the Earth was flat and that the Earth was the centre of the Universe because 'their God' said so – and thus arrived the Dark Ages, a retrogressive step if ever there was one!

It is only now, some 2,000 years later as we enter the Age of Aquarius, that we are beginning to rediscover the necessary respect for our Mother Earth. Material wealth has not provided the satisfaction we seek for it does not include that spiritual connection that was provided by paganism. Science, worshipped as a God but equally devoid of any spiritual connection, has provided us with the ability to free ourselves of many dreary chores and at the same time discovered the means for our very destruction.

Without the respect for Nature, Science has no qualms whatsoever to tamper with the very genetic basis that took Nature millennia to perfect. Science seems to believe that it can improve on Nature, yet over and over again we see that we are mistaken and behind the scenes short-sighted capitalists are simply exploiting and destroying the valuable resources that future generations will rely on for extraordinarily short-term gain. There are still many to discover that the pursuit of material wealth carries a false prophecy!

We must, however, not bury ourselves in all this talk of doom and gloom. There is hope and there are signs of profound change. The New Age of Aquarius is awakening in many that balance between the masculine and feminine. The male dominated dogma of the last few thousand years is gradually being put behind us. Modern Society is beginning to recognise that nurture and respect bears fruit far sweeter than bullish domination. Those who lead the way towards material enrichment for the few have, to necessitate their own ambitions, worked their way into power positions from which it is difficult to remove them – difficult, but not impossible. The magic and spirituality of the New Age will usurp these positions of power – why? – because we'll make sure of it!

One doesn't need to be a scientist to recognise the superiority of vegetables grown organically, planted in the right seasons in the correct phases of the moon and tenderly nourished with love and care. One doesn't need to be a scientist, one merely needs eyes, tastebuds and observation of how the body is enriched by eating such food. We will discover that we don't need the ludicrous promises made by the multi-national food corporations that genetic modification is the way forward to feed the world's population. Carefully planned and controlled debt is what causes poverty though it serves the capitalist systems of the West very well, at least in the short-term. Nature's own diversification can provide more than enough healthy food, as the struggling farmers in developing countries know only too well. They have not been debilitated to the same degree as those of us in developing countries by the quick fix solutions promised by science as they have remained closer to nature and understand its needs and requirements much better than us. If only they were allowed to get on with looking after themselves without interference from us in the West then they may well end up re-educating and teaching us in many otherwise forgotten agricultural applications.

When we rediscover the beauty that the Earth provides all around us, when we open our eyes and hearts to the wonders of Nature on our doorsteps we will begin to learn that whizzing past it all at a hundred miles an hour, polluting the air we breathe and damaging the very fabric of the planet's fragile eco-system in the process, is unnecessary and self defeating. We can retune ourselves to the beauty found in our own gardens, parks and woodlands. We will demand that trees be replanted and grown for their own sake, not simply as an exploitable resource, but for their own grace and magnificence as well as for the lungs they provide the Earth and the enriching spirit that they provide us.

As the influence of the new Aquarian Age grows, more and more people of all ages are seeking and beginning to find a newly inspired spirituality. The state control-inspired Christian church has, as the Piscean age fades, clearly lost its grip and influence even though it has made some effort to adapt. Whilst many have rejected any sense of spirituality and describe themselves as atheist, a spiritual aspect is vital if a great void in one's life is to be avoided as I believe a spiritual foundation is a fundamental element within a human life. The new age spirituality that many are seeking is an attempt to fill this void. It would appear vital that all spiritual paths, new or old, need to foster a respect for nature and a respect for ourselves, as an inseperable and interdepedent element of nature.

There is, however, little 'new' about the new spirituality that many are turning too. It has its roots in the ancient past, many thousands of years before Christianity forced its way onto the shores of Britain. It is an entirely natural religion that connects with the Earth and the

Cosmos and teaches a healthy balance between masculine and feminine – a balance missing throughout the Age of Pisces. It is the paganism that the Christian church tried to wipe out because it teaches individual empowerment – an anarchistic tendency that doesn't serve the masters of the Church. Despite mass persecution, the transformation of pagan deities into Christian saints, and the attempt to take over sites of worship, paganism could never be completely wiped out. Why? Because paganism is a natural religion and the individual and group psyche will automatically seek what feels natural and comfortable given a chance.

Paganism was the first form of spirituality that developed amongst our ancestors. It developed the way it did because there was no mass control over what people should believe in. Therefore they followed their instincts which is a far more reliable way to connect with the spirit without and within.

The early 'new age pioneers' such as Blavatsky looked towards Eastern religions such as Bhuddism and its many offshoots to find a more balanced and peaceful spirituality to blend with Christian values and concepts. There is much comfort and wisdom to be found through such teachings, but the Eastern ways do not always find an entirely comfortable position in the Western mind due to cultural differences. Generally speaking, the Eastern ways encourage their followers to bow down to a 'master'; in the West we find it more acceptable to learn how to become our own master. Neither way is right or wrong, just different and suitable to the cultures from which they come. Much has been learnt, however, from Eastern philosophy and a general blending of techniques has been a common theme through many new and revived esoteric traditions. Some have adopted, with varying degrees of success, a Buddhist path, others have revived and modernised those associated with mystical Christian, Judaic and Islamic paths and there are a whole range of neopagan revivals including druidry and witchcraft. One of the most exciting variations of the witchcraft revivals, and the theme of this book, is that of Wicca which, quite rightly, has been referred to as the only religion (or spiritual path) that Britain has offered the rest of the world and is said to be the fastest growing religion of the modern age.

Until 1951 witchcraft was still illegal in England and Wales (it still is in Scotland!). The law was not changed until members of the Spiritualist Church challenged the imprisonment of one of their number under this law for receiving 'channelled' information regarding matters that the Government considered 'top secret' with regard to World War two. Once this archaic law had been reformed and witchcraft was no longer illegal, those who had still been practising the Craft, and thus preserving it in one form or another, were able to start coming out of the woodwork.

One of the first of these was Gerald Gardner[4], a man from the Isle of Man who had been initiated into a New Forest coven in the south of England in the 1940s. He was a man who had studied many forms of spirituality and a great variety of magical traditions as had others he worked with including Doreen Valiente. Gardner drew much from the works of occultists such as Aleister Crowley, Charles Leyland and the published material of the Golden Dawn. He was a member of Aleister Crowley's magical order and was asked to continue his work after Crowley's death in 1947, though this offer was not taken up; Gardner had his own vision. What was eventually presented as a neo-pagan form of witchcraft, what we call Wicca today, was a blend of folk magic, traditional witchcraft and the more formal approach to Circle work more akin to that which is found in Druidry, Freemasonry and the Western Hermetic Tradition and incorporated some of the Eastern techniques for connecting with the higher self such as meditation. The law against witchcraft removed, a number of people began to come forward claiming a traditional or hereditary link to the Craft who seemed to confirm that at least some of the old ways had been kept alive behind the scenes.

Gerald Gardner's modern version of witchcraft, a group initiatory system, started to spread its influence. Some, such as Alex Sanders[5], developed it in his own way (a common theme to be encouraged within an individualistic tradition), others such as Raymond Buckland (initiated into Gerald Gardner's coven by his High Priestess Lady Olwen in 1963) took the system to the USA where it has also developed in many and various ways suitable to the American culture.

With the coming new age of Aquarius beginning to have its effect in the 1960s, people became to seriously question modern values. The hippy movement challenged politicians in a way never seen before. Interest grew in environmentalism as a closer bond with nature began to make people question the way we treated our Mother planet. Feminists started taking even more action to assert that they have equal rights with male counterparts (a battle still not truly won even today). The Church had lost its way and was in serious decline leaving a serious void and a lack of spiritual meaning to existence that needed to be filled. Many people were beginning (and continue ever more so today) to question the authority of the state

---

[4] Gerald Gardner is widely accepted as being responsible for 're-introducing' witchcraft to the twentieth century through his first book *High Magic's Aid* and following publications such as *Witchcraft Today*. However, there have always been those practising witchcraft in various forms (more often as solitary and natural practitioners – or 'Hedgewitches') throughout the millennia.

[5] Alex Sanders developed the 'Alexandrian' branch of Wicca from the original form laid down by Gardner.

and the state controlled religions. Having found a spirit within many are looking to the distant past and finding that the feminine aspects, so profoundly important, were worshipped at least on an equal footing with the masculine to great effect in a partnership model of society rather than a dominator model. They have rejected the idea that materialism in itself brings the deep satisfaction that they truly desire and that loving oneself and caring and nurturing for those around them and the environment in which we live can bring much greater rewards. The development of Wicca in recent decades readily provides a system that worships in the way when our ancestors were much more in tune with each other's needs and with the planet. It readily makes available a way of worshipping the divine feminine and masculine principles within nature and within each and every one of us. It is a system where one can truly discover the gods within and develop a way of tuning in to the other planes of existence that have been forgotten and neglected by society as a whole and using the energies there for a higher mission than mere material satisfaction.

Transformation of the individual is no easy task. Transformation of society as a whole is even harder and many will take a wrong step along the way. But each individual that discovers the gods within helps to transform that society in a small but important way, and those of us who feel the need to be there to help guide them on their way play an increasingly important role too. Wicca is just one way, of course. One that a growing number of people are discovering and adopting all over the Western world. However, Wicca does recognise that it has no exclusive claim to the path to enlightenment and revels in the great diversity of paths, thus accepting and welcoming other religious disciplines followed by those who resonate with other ways. There are today a great many definitions of what constitutes a modern-day 'pagan' and witch. Diversification is something that, in my opinion, is absolutely necessary and to be welcomed as it is vital that each system relates both to the individual, the culture in which the individual is brought up in, and the history of the individual's cultural group soul.

What follows is my own interpretation of modern Wicca. It is a system that follows a common theme within esoteric paths by starting with personal self development. It includes the more glamorous elements of witchcraft, such as spells and potions, but keeps them within the context of self development and spiritual growth. It is a system that has worked for me and is working for many of those who have come to me. It should be remembered, however, that whilst a great deal of knowledge can be found in a book, wisdom comes from the practical application of that knowledge and it is this practical application that will help you define your own individual way within the Craft.

4

IN THE BEGINNING

Celtic mythology does not provide us with a creation myth. It appears that the Celts didn't need one. The Celts believed in reincarnation and saw the soul as something that repeatedly went through the birth, life, death and rebirth cycle over and over, spending some time in what some called the Summerland. This was learnt and can be appreciated by witnessing and working with nature. It is the way the natural cycles work and therefore perfectly reasonable for cultures that maintained a close link with those cycles to build up such an understanding. The endless cycle is expressed in many ways through Celtic artwork – the Celtic knot which spirals around and around, weaving in and out of itself and never ending.

Wicca has drawn much from what has survived and learnt from the Celtic system, but has also accepted developments from other cultures as our ability to mingle and understand those cultures has grown throughout the millennia. A spiritual path that does not accept modernisation is one that is likely to be a victim of its own dogma. Unless spiritual understanding is allowed to develop organically, and move with the times, it is likely to become stale and irrelevant. Unless it is prepared to look at other belief systems and recognise that there are many paths that lead to the same goal – none necessarily right or wrong, simply different (though most will find that there is only one that feels right for themselves) – then there is an enormous risk of missing out on techniques and knowledge that bears an inner truth. Adaptability and evolution is something that is natural and serves nature well; we should understand that it will also serve our spiritual path well for the same reasons.

It is generally accepted within Wicca today that rather than a continuous and never ending cycle of death and rebirth, that the soul returns to the physical so that the soul can grow and perfect itself to a point where it no longer needs to return and can transcend into a spiritually evolved form to serve as part of the divine in other ways.

Whilst those who follow neo-pagan paths, including Wicca, respect the wisdom of their ancestors they are not all closed to new ideas, a matter that I consider to be an important aspect if paganism is to adapt to new and unforeseen circumstances and progressive understanding. The following is how I see the beginning of creation and fits in well, in my opinion, with the general modern pagan view:

In the beginning there was a mass of pure energy or light. The energy generated Force and Form, that which we refer to as God and Goddess, which caused manifestations of all kinds to burst into existence throughout the Cosmos. Naturally the form existed before the force animated it, otherwise there would have been nothing to animate, and nothing for the force emanate from. Energy cannot be created or destroyed only transformed. Everything that exists comes from the same source, be it animal, mineral or plant; spirit and matter, and therefore everything is inextricably connected.

The Force and Form that came from the ultimate source of power and energy sub-divided into various elements of Force and Form. These vibrations can be envisaged, through various names (and often visualised in appropriate anthropomorphic forms) as the many and varied Gods and Goddesses. Through opening ourselves to the inner truths that they represent, we can work with our Gods and Goddesses – with these natural energies – to transform for better or worse, good or bad. Our love and appreciation of the goddesses and gods that together represent elements of the divine source of which we are a part, propels us to work with them, and as part of them, to enhance and further their work.

Whilst being aware of these energies and having the confidence to work with them brings power, it is necessary to wield that power with respect. The energies can be worked without being fully in tune with them to a limited extent. However, with so many working energies in such a way, and for selfish and negative reasons, there is much work to do to obtain balance and harmony.

The Earth – born from the Ultimate Source – is our immediate Mother and deserves to be respected as such. From the moment of our conception on the physical plane she provides the nourishment for us to grow. When our physical bodies die we return to become part of the Earth again. Our Spirit (or Soul) however, is an element of the collective soul that is striving towards perfection and to reunite the various planes of existence. The Soul cannot be destroyed and through this we gain immortality. At present, however, it is only on the physical plane that the soul can learn, transform and grow. It is on the physical plane that it is able to gain experience which it then takes with it take add to previous experiences. When an individual Soul has learnt as much as it can it no longer reincarnates and rejoins the collective – though retaining 'memory' of its experiences which it is able to share with other souls, particularly those who are arranged in its own 'soul group'. Meditation and past life regression can help open ourselves up to our higher selves and the memories of experiences gained in the past (and for many work of that kind can help understand and correct apparent irrational response that are often the result of unconscious conditioning from those past lives).

Through reincarnation and return to the collective soul, through the lessons learned on the physical plane, we begin to bring the balance and harmony that is required to achieve the goal of creation – what some would call 'heaven on earth' or 'as above so below'. Each of us as physical individuals, it would seem, are here to learn lessons which we then take with us to the spiritual plane after our present incarnation has terminated in order to contribute a greater range of experiences and knowledge, firstly to our own soul energy and through that to a group of souls who we work with and share with, and through that to benefit the universal soul energy of which each of us is but a tiny fragment. In the spiritual plane we are unfettered by the often severe constraints imposed by the ego, are able to examine our experiences objectively and subjectively and able to measure our progress honestly and openly with understanding and without guilt. We shall know the good things we have done on the physical plane, as well as the bad things we have done and the mistakes we made, and be able to determine what we could do in order to do better next time, if indeed we have not yet reached a point where we are able to progress beyond the need to reincarnate more.

It is also my understanding that the source from which our soul energy originated also produces entities that do not enter into the human reincarnation process, but take a different course and serve in other ways. These spirits would explain the force within the forms of trees, crystals, etc and other physical forms as well as the spiritual aspects that manifest to some in the form of spirit guides (or 'angels') and the entities that are invoked as the elemental energies of earth, air, fire and water in a Circle. This is a large subject in its own right, but if one works along any path of spiritual development, the truth of this may well become clear. Though the forms may manifest to each of us in different ways, depending on the path that has drawn us, the energy from which it emanates is inevitably the same.

The following charges of the Goddess and of the God (written by a modern Wiccan High Priestess) give us a typical introduction to the way we understand that the Celts lived their lives and the values that they held close to them . . .

ELEMENTS OF THE GODDESS[6]

The following verse describes the gifts given to us by the Goddess in Her Earth aspects. It charges us to challenge our mind (which will be discussed in detail in following chapters); charges us to 'strive always for the growth of your soul' and to use her energies ('powers') in her service until 'the last star darkens in the sky and winter comes to the universe'.

I am the petals of the rosebuds in Springtime
the warmth of the Sun in Summer
the softly dancing spirit of Autumn
the peace of the quiet woods
as the chill calms the Earth in Winter
I am the burst of song in
the morning
the gentle hand of the Maiden
and the deep river of the
mysteries taught by moonlight

I give the creatures of the earth
the gifts of song rising from the heart
the joy of autumn sunset
the cool touch of the renewing waters
and the compelling call of the drum in the dance

To you I give the joy of creation and the companion
of beauty to light your days

By the powers of the steadfast Earth
the glowing flame and the
shining stars I charge you
by the darkness of death
and the white light of birth I charge you
and through the perfect love and perfect trust
of those closest to you
I charge you

Strive always for the growth of your eternal soul
never intentionally diminish your strength
your compassion
your ties to the earth or your knowledge

---

[6] Traditional text – source unknown.

Challenge your mind
never accept complacency that which
has been the standard merely for the reason
that it is the standard
by which the majority rules itself

Thirdly I charge you
to act always for the betterment of your
brothers and sisters
To strengthen them is to forge the true chain
of humanity
and a chain is only as strong as its weakest link

You are my children
my brothers and sisters and my companions
You are known in great part
by the company you keep
and you are strong and wise
and full of the powers of life
It is yours to use them in my service
and I also
am known by the company I keep

Go forth in joy and the light of my love
turning to me
without fear when the darkness
threatens to overcome you
and turning also to me to share your triumphs
and your achievements
and know in your heart of hearts
that we are together in blood and spirit
till the last star
darkens in the sky and winter comes to the universe

SO IT MUST BE

ELEMENTS OF THE GOD[7]

The following 'Charge of the God' describes the energies of the male deity as God of Nature, God of the Sun and the Dark God of Death and rebirth. It describes how the God aspects relate to those of the

---

[7] Traditional text – source unknown.

Goddess and how the male energies of force bring forth form from the female energies.

I am the fleet deer in the forest,
I am the beach which receives the waves,
I am the sun which warms the earth.
I am the Lord of the Spiral Dance of Life,
Death and Rebirth,
the gentle reaper,
the Winter stag and the Spring fawn.
All things are of me,
for I am of the Goddess,
opposite, yet not opposing.
I bring birth forth from the womb that is a tomb,
for I am the seed which fertilises.
I am abundant Life,
for I am the grain that grows and I am death,
the harvest in the Fall.
And I am rebirth after darkness,
for I am the seed that springs forth anew.

I am fertility,
the spreader of Life,
and I am the Lord of Death,
which adds value to life.
I am the Guardian of the Gate between Life and Death.
I am King of the Underworld,
where no living being may venture,
but I am also the King of Rebirth,
turning the tomb into a womb.

I bring love and strength,
peace and passion,
hope and joy,
for I am the gentle lover in the night.
All that I am comes from the Great Mother,
the Divine Star Goddess,
who is Mother of us all.

5

MEDITATION (PART ONE)

A disciplined and daily routine of meditation is an essential element to spiritual growth. This is something that many will find difficult to fit into to the modern hectic lifestyle, though paradoxically something that will infinitely help us cope with it too. It is the connection made through the subconscious during meditation that we begin to discover our higher selves[8]. It is through this discovery that we find the key to unlock the boundaries between the physical plane and the other planes that at first remain unseen but are part of the key to future magical work. It is our link to that which takes care of our spiritual well-being and retains our 'universal memory'. Meditation opens the door to personal spiritual growth, psychic development and all that there is beyond what we perceive as the extremely limited reality in our normal everyday lives.

Meditation comes easier to some than others, though everyone can do it and get better at it with practice. There are many forms of meditation and many methods are taught, none particularly more or less valid than any others, although some techniques will suit us better as individuals than others. Most techniques have their roots in eastern traditions but are often easily adapted for use in any spiritual path.

At first it would be best to simply use meditation purely for relaxing, clearing one's mind of the day to day clutter of modern living and using it to visualise a clear and empty space. Once this has been achieved one can go with the flow of any images that come up of their own accord. Meditation can be used to focus on issues and, once a technique is fully developed, can lead on to contemplation through which comes a new and clear connection, through one's higher self.

Some techniques employ the use of a mantra that is chanted. This may be of some use for those who have trouble learning how to

---

[8] 'Higher self' can also be described as the 'inner self', 'spiritual consciousness', 'super conscious', 'creative force' and many other names. Whatever term is used it is basically the same, though the super conscious is more correctly applied to the fully opened channel to the whole soul, rather than an element of it.

meteate[9], and is a way of shutting out the conscious mind and the chatter that often accompanies it. By focusing on a mantra you are, however, not fully allowing the space for the subconscious thought forms to flow so I feel the use of such techniques has limitations.

During meditation the brain enters an altered state of consciousness – known as 'alpha' – a state also entered during deep relaxation and dreaming. In the alpha state the brain waves register at between seven and fourteen cycles[10]. This is close to the background energy cycles of the Earth itself.

Through practice, work in the alpha state can open one up to a whole new, much broader, sense of reality then hitherto discovered. Not only can one benefit enormously from temporarily by-passing the glamours of the ego to gain contact and communication with one's higher self, but one is also better able to develop skills such as telepathy, clairvoyance and pre-cognition. It is in the alpha state that we are able to enter and explore the other planes of reality that include the astral and spiritual planes creating a situation where we are much more open and receptive to the energies that exist all around us, rather just those on the more commonly recognised physical plane.

Alpha is a state where we can expand into the vibrationary rates of the other planes of existence. It is whilst working between these planes where much of the occult work is undertaken – which will be discussed more fully later in this book.

Meditation is basically the means by which we gain access to the quantum reality; a greater sense of the breadth of reality than we are commonly aware of as a young adolescent, or even as an adult if we haven't explored beyond the materialistic physical plane. Visualisation work during meditation is a vital element in magic whether it be used, as many do, for healing purposes or other intentions.

Another technique for those who may struggle with meditations, or even for the more advanced who want to work on specific issues or courses of action, is a guided meditation. This is best carried out with somebody you trust and who knows what they are doing as it can involve going much deeper than you would usually delve on your own, although one can have some success using pre-recorded tapes

---

[9] It would be advisable to steer clear of any teachers using a system that leads on to a specific spiritual teaching that is not necessarily of your own choosing. Having had personal experience of Transcendental Meditation in my youth I remain deeply suspicious of the motives of those who teach that particular technique.

[10] When mentally alert the brain registers at fourteen to thirty cycles per second – known as Beta. The slower rate of four to seven cycles per second, associated with drowsiness and euphoria, is known as Theta, whilst the Delta state of deep dreamless sleep works at one to three cycles per second.

(preferably those you have prepared yourself). You can learn to use such techniques to reach the higher self where past life memories reside. You will discover that it is here that we can discover many of the blockages and fears that affect our current incarnation.

Having mastered basic meditation techniques, the next step is to start working on visualisations. Starting with simple objects such as a burning candle, or an apple, one can gradually start building up quite complex images. Once mastered, one can continue to use meditation as a door to the astral plane that can be used for all sorts of work including building your own personal temple that can become your own private and personal space. This will be discussed in more detail in a later chapter.

The first thing to do when preparing to meditate is find a suitable location. If it is warm and sunny, and you have access to the countryside, or even a decent park, sitting under a tree or among flowers can be very invigorating. At home, finding a quiet place to sit, either in a comfortable chair or on the floor, is ideal. Sitting in front of your altar can be quite inspiring. It is important that you are not going to be disturbed, so take the phone off the hook, turn any mobile phones off too, and if you share the house with others let them know what you are doing and that you would appreciate it if you are not disturbed. Having a phone ring, or a child shout in your ear once deep in meditation, can be quite disturbing to say the least.

Make sure that you sit comfortably. Many people like to sit crossed-legged or in a lotus position (as in Eastern techniques) but this is far from essential. The important thing is that you are comfortable, and that you sit upright with your spine straight so that the energies can flow through your body uninhibited; the posture is very important as it helps us to breathe properly and breath control is a key element in most techniques. If sitting in a chair it is good to use an upright chair with a high back. If sitting on the floor it is a good idea to use a cushion or two. You can meditate laying flat on your back if you prefer, though this may lead to you fall asleep which is not entirely desirable and therefore not recommended.

SIMPLE MEDITATION TECHNIQUE

Make yourself comfortable having taken the precautions mentioned above. Close your eyes. Take a few moments to allow your mind to settle and take a deep breath in through your nose filling up the deepest levels of your lungs first, then your chest, right in a far as you can. Hold the breath for a second, then breath out slowly and thoroughly. Take a second deep breath and as you do so see light filling your body and then breath out slowly through your mouth visualising all the dark negative energies within being expelled from your body. Do this for a third time.

After the third breath allow your mind to go blank and allow your breathing to settle into a gentle and natural rhythm. Try to focus on a point between your eyebrows and about an inch inside your head and visualise a simple blank white piece of paper. If other images appear, allow them to develop and then bring your mind back to the blank sheet of paper. Do not worry about letting your mind wander too much, but if you find yourself mulling over the stresses of the day then recognise that this is your conscious mind at work and gently put those thoughts to one side and bring yourself back to the centre.

Allow this continue for some time. This could be anything from five minutes to half and hour or more. There is no need to set a time limit as such and better not to enter a meditation with a set time schedule in mind.

When you feel you are ready, start to take deep breathes again, breathing deeply as before. Gently open your eyes and continue to breath steadily until you are ready to stand up and get on with the rest of the day. You should by this point feel much calmer and relaxed.

This is a very basic form of meditation. It is one that needs to be properly mastered before moving on to techniques that involve visualisation, and from there beyond to contemplative methods and astral travel. All of these more advanced techniques begin in the same way as above with the breathing exercises and centring on the third eye.

To take the meditation one stage further, one can begin to develop concentration more by putting some words – the focus of the meditation – on the sheet of paper. Repeat the words over and over and gradually concentrate fully on the meaning of the words, their significance and implications. Continue doing this until the meaning is clear and you find that you are no longer actually looking at the form of words themselves.

You will find that trying to rush meditation will lead to disappointment. It is something that you need to develop over a long time scale, perhaps several years. Perseverance is the key. Benefits will be felt from the beginning, but the deeper revelations may take a little longer. The best time to meditate is first thing in the morning. This will enable you start the day off centred spiritually and will help you undertake the day's work, whatever that might be, in a manner that is far more productive and free of stress. However, if one simply cannot find the time in the morning, then that is not a reason not to find time later in the day.

Ensure that you set aside a special time and place for yourself for this work. You deserve to make the time for yourself even though many will find all sorts of excuses such as being too busy. It does not take much to find a mere twenty minutes a day for meditation work. It may mean missing out on a few of the more mundane parts of one's day, or even getting up just a little earlier in the mornings, but if one is serious about developing one's spiritual aspects then meditation is an essential element that simply cannot be missed.

GROUNDING

At the end of any meditation, and even more so with one of the more advanced techniques, it is important to ensure that you are properly and fully grounded.

Grounding is a way of ensuring that any excess energies that have been accessed through meditation are returned to the earth rather than left buzzing around one's system – it works in a similar fashion to a grounding wire in a electrical system. After bringing oneself out of the meditation, after resuming normal breathing, with your feet on the ground one can simply visualise excess energy flowing into the earth for a few moments. If this does not seem to be enough, then kneel on the floor and put your palms flat on the ground and do the same.

Eating a dry biscuit, or something similar, and taking a drink can help this process considerably. You will notice (later in this book) that at the end of most of the ceremonies and rituals used within a Circle situation, there is a ceremony that is used called the 'cakes and wine'. The cake represents the body of the Goddess and the wine her blood, but it is also included for purposes of grounding as above.

HEALING MEDITATION

Healing of oneself and others is a practice that many witches involve themselves in. It is just one way of sharing the gifts one is developing. Many may find that sharing this ability to channel – or more accurately 'direct' – healing energy is a calling in itself and may not find a desire to use their esoteric development for anything else. There is certainly nothing wrong with that. In the modern physical world there is certainly enough healing required to keep us all busy throughout our current lives and beyond.

Meditation techniques can be used by an individual, or as guided meditation led by a nominated person, in a group situation. What follows here is a simple meditation visualisation designed to help send natural healing energies to those who are in need. It is always good practice to do this for people who have asked for help, or people with whom you have discussed and told what you are doing for them.

During this meditation you are introduced to the concept of drawing energy from both the Earth and from the infinite divine light energy above. This is a fundamental element in healing and is similar to the techniques used by those who have learnt the Eastern method of Reiki healing as well as others. You are also introduced here to visualisation, the concept of chakras and auras, more of which we shall discuss later. During this meditation you will be asked to stimulate all of your senses, a technique that helps to strengthen the visualisation. Whilst you may, at first, feel a little tired after this sort of work (this is quite normal and should soon pass) if you were to send healing energy purely from yourself then you would end up completely drained and leave yourself open to requiring healing yourself.

You can use the following either by having somebody read it out to you while you meditate, or record it in your own voice and play the tape back. Remember to leave plenty of space between each line in order to carry out the instruction. This meditation is particularly suited for working in a group situation.

Make sure you are comfortable . . .
As you slow your breathing you are perfectly calm and relaxed . . .
We are standing in an ancient stone circle, facing each other. There is soft fine grass between us, lichen growing on the old silver-grey stones . . .
There is the sweet scent of lavender in the air . . .
Invite your friendly spirit guides and helpers to join us if they wish . . .
As we breathe gently, we notice the air is fresh and clear . . .
As we breathe in, we breathe clear cleansing light, purifying our body, clearing our mind. As we breathe out we let any dark impurity expel itself from our body . . .
Around our circle there is a mysterious gentle mist. We hear the birds cheerfully chirping . . .
. . . we hear rabbits running around playfully. This is a peaceful place . . .
The grass sparkles with little diamonds of dew. Feel the grass between your toes . . .
Open the soles of your feet to open to the earth and begin to feel the energy rise up in you . . .
Feel your connection with the earth . . . Draw from deep down like the roots of a great oak tree . . .
As the energy builds up in you, open your crown chakra to the abundant Universal energy from above
The golden Universal light floods into your crown, mixing with the earth energies . . . allow it to flow out of your heart chakra into the middle of our circle . . .

A bright glow builds up in the circle and begins to get brighter and brighter . . .
It is now so bright and powerful that it extends beyond us, beyond our circle . . .
As we keep the energy flowing, the light dissolves the mist and sweeps across green valleys and hills . . .
The healing light sweeps across rivers and seas to everyone who has asked for help . . .
See those people surrounded by our golden healing light, bringing peace and calm to their lives . . . see them smile . . .
As we draw yet more energy, the light continues to sweep across the planet, bringing peace and harmony to every place it reaches . . .
The healing energy helps those involved in conflict find peaceful solutions, it brings an end to pain and sorrow in the world and eases the suffering of all life – plant and animal . . .
As the energy continues to grow and the light intensifies further we move out to the stars above and look back at our home floating through space like a bright jewel in the Universe . . .
See the planet glow, like a bright star . . . surrounded by a golden halo
Keep the energy flowing . . . see the bright glow and feel the love and pure joy embrace our Earth . . .
Now, when you are ready, gently let the light begin to subside . . .
See the energy settle where it is most needed . . .
In your own time, come back to our circle . . .
Feel your gentle, deep breathing again . . .
Send any remaining energy back down the roots to the earth, saving enough for your own needs . . .
It is a bright summers day . . . feel the beautifully fresh air fill your lungs . . .
Thank your guides and helpers. Let them know they are free to stay or leave . . .
Seal your aura. You are a creature of beauty and light . . .
Blessings be to one and all.

TREE MEDITATION

The following can be either used for the basis of a meditation, or read before a general meditation to contemplate on, or better still, go out into the garden, park or countryside and stand in front of a real tree . . .

Pick a tree. Any tree. It can be a noble oak, a magnificent beech, or a humble apple. Stand in front of this tree and study it.

The tree's roots venture deep into the Earth from where it draws sustenance. It needs water and minerals that it uses to build itself and grow; just as you do. When you eat and drink you take into your body physical matter that your own body uses to grow and renew itself as cells continually die and regenerate; just as the tree does. The matter that you take into your body comes from the Earth through the vegetables you eat either directly, or via the animals that ate them before you. The same matter that the tree is drawing from to live.

The soil is made from matter that has been part of many living organisms, in one form or another, and has returned to the soil to be broken to continue the cycle of life, death and rebirth. The matter that makes up the physical tree comes from the same place as that which you are made of – our Mother Earth. The matter may once have sustained other organisms, our ancestors. The tree is your kin, honour it as such.

Stand in front of the tree and imagine roots spreading down deep into the Earth. Feel the energy as it rises in you. This energy feeds and nurtures. The tree is constantly in touch with this life-giving energy, just as you are. It can be drawn upon at any time.

The tree also draws energy from above. In order to transform that which it draws from below, it requires energy from the sun; just as you do. When you eat and drink you take in matter that requires energy from above to transform it into a form that can be utilised by your body. You also draw energy from above directly through your skin to help produce sustenance in the forms of vitamins. The energy from above that helps bring life to everything on the Earth comes from the same source – the Sun. Just as the Earth can be seen as our Mother, she could not bear life without the Sun that can be seen, in the same way, as our Father. Such is the duality of things.

Stand in front of the tree and whilst feeling the energy rise from deep below, also feel the energy drawing down from above through your crown just as the tree does through its leaves. This energy can also be drawn upon at any time.

Honour your Mother and Father – they bring life to you and everything around you.

But don't let this consideration stop there. The matter that makes up the Earth and the Sun, indeed every planet in this solar system, every other system, every galaxy – the entire Universe – has a common source. At one point everything that makes up material existence came from a single source – of which we, the tree, and everything else are a mere fragment, constantly moving from one form to another. This is what some describe as the Divine Source (there are many names) from which came, by some means or another, our Mother Earth and Father Sun and which in turn made us possible as well as everything else in the physical Universe. Under-standably many see the Earth as a Goddess and the Sun as a God; between them they give us physical life and sustain us until we die after which our body is returned to the Earth.

Matter is generally that which is perceivable by the five commonly recognised senses of touch, taste, smell, sight and hearing. The five senses experience a tiny proportion of that which exists. Human sight is limited to a very narrow range of vibrating waves. Hearing is limited in exactly the same way. It is easy to understand how many fail to look beyond that which is material.

However, what is matter? Look between the spaces of what you perceive as the physical reality and you will discover a great deal more.

6

SELF DEVELOPMENT

As has already been said, witchcraft is primarily a religious undertaking within the realms of the neopagan community.

It is through this faith, understanding and the reconnection with nature that one begins to re-experience the natural energies that have always been around us, but have become largely ignored in the modern world. Witchcraft is secondarily a method of self-development, or self-transformation and as such (if one chooses to go further) a step towards working as a magician and thus help others, the environment on which we depend and as part of a 'team' with others in the spiritual plane.

One can achieve what the alchemist is aiming for when trying to transform lead into gold, or the Kabbalist when climbing the tree of life. It is only after one has taken a large step down the spiral path (as depicted below) and started on one's way back again that one should even start to consider doing any serious magical work beyond developing oneself. However, as the connection with the higher self does develop one begins to see quite clearly that the self that has been experienced to date in the physical form is much deeper that first imagined. One starts to get in touch with one's higher purpose in life, the gradual perfection of the soul which houses many life memories, and beyond that the gradual transformation of the collective conscious towards its own goal.

The path of the Wiccan is an initiatory path that begins with self development and ultimately aims to complete the path, as all esoteric traditions do, by connecting with the divine. It is once that connection has been made that the real work starts. Magic is about transforming energies for the common good, and one is only able to fully appreciate what constitutes the common good, and tap into the most potent energies fully, when one has become fully connected. That is not to say that there is not a great deal one can do in the meantime. Having chosen to step on to the path in the first place and work on oneself is ultimately for the common good and connecting with natural energies by appreciating nature and celebrating the wheel of the year helps in itself to open up energy channels that all will benefit from.

There is much that is misunderstood about witchcraft that needs to be corrected whenever the opportunity arises. This is not entirely surprising when one sees books in shops by 'publicity witches' and TV programs such as 'Sabrina the Teenage Witch'. It is pleasing to see that witches are now being presented in a way that helps to counteract the image of a sickly green warty old woman casting evil spells. However, it is so sad when people hear about Wicca or witchcraft, and express an interest in it, to discover that actually all they want is to be able to work a 'love spell' or a 'money spell'. I fear that the growth of Wicca is largely due to the false impression that the Craft can be used to embellish oneself materially and manipulate others. This could not be more wrong! Fortunately unless one is prepared to put in the work to transform and retune oneself, then the elements that make magic work will elude those who believe it to be a technique for material gratification.

SO WHERE DOES ONE START ON THE PATH TO SELF-DEVELOPMENT?

The place to start is to look closely at your lifestyle, consider what is good in your life, what you really value, whether what you value really enhances your life and thus is actually of true value. Contemplate and consider what you feel is missing.

You must learn to truly love yourself, because if you don't love yourself you cannot possibly expect others to love you, and you can't possibly spread the love you have of life to the outside community if the love of yourself is not apparent. This does not mean that you need to become arrogant and self-righteous. None of us are perfect, but it is recognising those imperfections and working on them, and not judging oneself hard for accepting that you are not perfect that is important.

When you fall in love, the world is full of magic. When you learn to love yourself you will find that the magic comes from within. When you discover the Universe is full of magic you fall in love with all that it has to offer and begin to live life to the full.

Self-development is a concept that is fundamental to all esoteric traditions throughout history. Ancient drawings representing the spiral path (figure 1) have been found at sites all across the world from times when no physical contact could possibly have been made to spread the universality of this symbol. Glastonbury Tor in Somerset, England (for example), from the foot of which this book was written, includes an ancient path cut physically into the hillside, walking in and out of

▲ *Figure 1 – The Cretan Maze or spiral path.*

which one feels a sense of great power and of treading a path that has been trod by many initiates throughout the millennia.

The inward spiral represents an inner voyage of discovery. One follows this path to discover the inner realities of one's own existence to the centre, and having found the centre one starts on the outer spiral path of development, bringing with you those inner discoveries, and from which you emerge transformed. One may well find that one enters and walks out of this spiral several times in one's life. The initiation process of the Craft described later in this book very much marks the transit through this form of development. The spiral path, or maze, involves seven levels that must be walked before one reaches the centre that correspond to the seven planes (although there are many other interpretations) which will be discussed more fully in chapter 8 on *The Otherworld*.

▲ *Glastonbury Tor.*

One word of warning at this stage. Many people who have become adept at magic have been through severe traumas in their lives. This may be something physical that could possibly have left one injured, or a deep emotional trauma that leaves one injured in another way. Such points in one's life can become great turning points as one delves deep into oneself to discover the true meaning of life. Treading a path of self-development can uncover aspects of one's past that one hasn't necessarily faced and which need to be dealt with in order to move forward. This in itself can be a very painful and emotional experience, but one which can be deeply rewarding in the long term. Without walking into the darkest places of our mind and facing our deepest fears and dealing with them we cannot possibly hope to fully appreciate and celebrate the joy of living. The more one experiences the dark, the more one appreciates the light. I would not want anyone to think that walking such a path is easy. The rewards are great indeed, but hard work is necessary in order to earn those rewards.

Self development leaves us in a state of heightened awareness. In such a state we become far more sensitive to the energies around us, to the energies emanating from ourselves and from others. This increased sensitivity needs to be controlled and contained. Therefore do not rush your self development. Allow time for your mind to adjust to the increased sensitivity and learn how to contain it. Even at an advanced level of development it is easy to fall off the tightrope. Balance is everything if you don't want to fall and get lost in the darkness or drunk in the light. You may well find that having undertaken this work that you feel times of stagnation. This is usually the time your mind is taking to readjust. This is not a time to stop the meditation work, but a time we need to persevere. The development will continue when every-thing settles naturally and is ready to move on to the next stage.

You can use your meditation work, which I would advise is done at least on a daily basis, to start connecting with the higher self. Meditation work should be part of your daily routine. It is a time for yourself, and if you can't spare fifteen or twenty minutes a day on yourself then I would suggest there is something very seriously wrong with your life style that needs to be addressed.

You can also use the following affirmation, or one of your own devising, on a daily basis. Sit or stand in front of the mirror and recite the following words:

I am unique.
There is no one else exactly like me.
And yet I am one with the whole of Nature.
I have the right to be what I am.

My essential self is divine and beautiful.
I have the right also to be better than I am,
that the outer manifestation may be more true to the inner reality.
May the Goddess and God of all creation
grant me beauty in the inward soul,
and may the outward and the inward life be as one.[11]

Having read those words, read them again and reflect on their meaning. Use the affirmation, or something like it of your own devising that you feel fully comfortable with, regularly to ensure that this is kept at the forefront of your mind. Repetition is a technique used in many traditions, as is the use of poetic verse and chanting, as a way of transferring an idea from the conscious firmly into the sub-conscious. How often have you found yourself with a song rattling around in your mind, even a song that you don't particularly like? This is because the form of rhythm and verse are attracted to the sub-conscious. Having recognised the truth of this, use the method for your own benefit.

WORDS OF POWER

Words of Power are a form of verse that can be used in your work on self-development as a form of prayer, within meditations, or incorporated for use within Circle work. They can be used in a similar fashion to the affirmation shown above. They are repeated on a regular basis until the thought form reaches the sub-conscious and beyond and begins to manifest with force into the physical again.

There is a general formula that you can use to build your own Words of Power to be used either to work on negative aspects within yourself, or to develop positive ones.

The general pattern is to start off with an affirmation that you recognise the divine, and yourself as part of the divine. You could therefore start with words such as . . .

Lady and Lord, Goddess and God,
I am of you as you are of me.

You can then continue by defining the element of the divine that you wish to attain or strengthen within yourself. This could be an attribute such as harmony or love. To strengthen this attribute one could include an image to aid the visualisation. So one could continue . . .

---

[11] With apologies to Marion Weinstien on whose words these are based.

You bless us with the peace and harmony,
Of flowering meadows in the heat of summer.

You then embrace that image, that is an element of the divine. You have already confirmed that you are part of the divine, you therefore proceed by affirming this attribute as part of yourself too . . .

I embrace this peace and harmony,
And draw it into myself.

You complete the Words of Power with a positive statement of intent that that attribute is yours, as a right and at this moment in time, that it is according to the free will of all (ie that you are not depriving others of a similar right) and that it is so . . .

Right here, right now,
For the good of all,
According to the free will of all,
So it must be!

The last line is an affirmation that you have concluded the work. (Variations on 'So it must be' include: 'And so it is' or 'And so is it' or 'And this is so' or 'So mote it be'.[12]) Incidentally, the affirmation that traditionally ends a Christian prayer – 'Amen' – means much the same (strangely invoking an Egyptian deity, though that is another story). The important thing is that you don't choose a concluding statement that implies doubt, such as 'I hope it is so.'

To put the whole verse, prayer or affirmation together we end up with . . .

Lady and Lord, Goddess and God,
I am of you as you are of me.
You bless us with the peace harmony,
Of flowering meadows in the heat of summer.
I embrace this peace and harmony,
And draw it into myself.
Right here, right now,
For the good of all,
According to the free will of all,
So it must be!

Continue to focus on the words representing the attributes you desire by repeating them over and over, in this case 'peace and

---

[12] 'So mote it be' is a traditional Wiccan affirmation taken from Old English literally meaning 'So it must be'.

harmony', and as you do so allow the visual representation of those words (the flowering meadow in the heat of summer) to grow in your mind until you can actually see and feel the peace and harmony which you are claiming as yours.

As with all prayers, affirmations and rituals, feel free to adapt such words to suit yourself. It is important that such words flow, and that they have meaning to yourself and the way you see the divine. Blindly following someone else's words is futile unless you fully understand the meaning and the meaning is true to your understanding and tradition. It is the general formula and elements of the content that are the vital things to remember, not these particular words in themselves.

Please note, especially if you are developing your own form of words, that in these affirmations and Words of Power that we do not use any negatives. This is an important point to remember. The subconscious will pick up and dwell on negatives, even if used in a form where a double negative is used to create a positive. Therefore we would not say: 'I am not a bad person' but instead would use 'I am a good person' in its place.

CHAKRAS

Balancing oneself can be achieved through meditation and by working with what is known in Eastern traditions as the Chakra points. There are seven of these points in our bodies which funnel out beyond our physical frame into our aura. They also have correspondences to the seven planes of existence.

The base chakra, also known as the 'kundalini', is at the bottom of your spine. The kundalini is portrayed as a coiled serpent that, as one develops, gradually uncoils itself winding up around the other chakra points into one's mind and beyond. The second chakra is the spleen, a point just below or at your belly button. The third is your solar plexus, a point low in the your chest just above your stomach and below the sternum. The forth chakra is your heart, the fifth your throat, sixth your third eye between your eyebrows and slightly above. The final seventh chakra comes out of the top of your head – your crown.

The chakras correspond with the colours of the rainbow. Red is at the base going through to orange for your spleen, yellow for your solar plexus turning to green for your heart, light blue at your throat to dark blue or indigo at your third eye before becoming violet through your crown. You can visualise these colours rising up through your body during meditation sessions. See the energy uncoiling itself from the base of your spine, curling up through your body winding around each chakra point until it bursts with energy through the top of your head.

The aura around the body is part of your etheric projection. Many people will begin to see auras when they are on the road to self development. Some see them easier than others, but everyone it seems has the ability. The colours projected can reflect your state of mind or mood at any moment. Working on the chakra points will help to strengthen your aura.

Using crystals can add extra power to a chakra meditation and can help the balancing process considerably. Lie comfortably on the floor or on your bed, preferably naked (skyclad). If you have a partner then begin a gentle meditation and ask them to place the crystals on your chakra points, otherwise you will need to place them yourself beforehand. Feel the energy from the crystals and gradually let this energy flow up from the base of your spine as before. Use crystals that have good healing qualities and which correspond in colour to the chakra colours mentioned above. I use a red tiger's eye or red jasper for the base chakra; an orange carnelian for the spleen; a honey calcite for the solar plexus; a green bloodstone (with a splash of red) for the heart; a light blue-lace agate for the throat; a deep blue sodalite or lapis lazuli for the third eye and an amethyst for the top of the head. Additional energy can be added using other clear quartz crystal points placed around the body and pointing inwards. Don't overdo it, however, the energy from crystals can be quite strong!

TUNING YOUR BODY AND MIND IN WITH NATURE

Working out of doors with natural energies of trees and plants, as well as the underlying natural earth energy that flows from below is an enriching experience that you should also aim to incorporate into your development work. One can learn a lot by simply looking closely at flowers that you find in the fields or hedgerows. If nothing else, the pure beauty of nature is an enriching experience in itself. If you live in a city then there are always parks where you can sit for a moment and escape from the hustle and bustle of streets full of cars and lorries.

The Celts, who inspired a great deal of modern Wicca, saw themselves and their gods fully integrated with nature, rather than being nature's master or adversary which seems to be the common misconception.

Learn to recognise the different varieties of trees and wild flowers. If you are not sure about them, buy yourself a little identification book listing all of your native trees and wild flowers. As well as being an enjoyable hobby, it will also help bring the bond with nature closer to you. Many of the herbs found in fields and hedgerows, parks and gardens referred to as 'weeds' actually turn out to be species that can be used in herbalism. Be careful what you pick: there may well be laws against picking wild flowers in your country. Some may be poisonous, so be thoroughly certain what you have picked before you put it to use.

A lot can also be learnt from the way trees and plants grow, and how each has adapted to the situation it has found itself in. A tree on a steep hillside, for instance, may have extended its roots in order to provide it with more stability. An exposed tree on a hill or cliff top may have learnt to grow in a way that it is in sympathy with the strong prevalent wind rather than growing straight as its species would normally do. By examining these species and meditating with them it is possible to learn many simple, yet often pertinent, lessons that we can apply in our daily lives.

Let nature be your teacher and you shall certainly become wise.

In years past there would have been a far greater variety of wild herbs; herbicides used on farms have wiped a lot of them out and made once common species quite rare. Village witches would have built up a broad knowledge of the medicinal uses of herbs at the very least and there are still many available that work as well as, if not better than the drugs prescribed by a doctor. In fact, many of today's drugs are synthetic copies of herbs that have been used throughout the ages (though far more expensive and often with extraordinary and dubious side effects).

Many of these herbs and flowers can also be utilised in the making of incense for occult work. If you learn the correspondences of each plant then you can incorporate them into your work bringing an additional dimension to the all-important associations.

As well as looking out for trees and plants, look out for the wildlife that surrounds you. I would venture to suggest that the vast majority of those living around you are totally ignorant of the great variety of wildlife, including insects, birds, fish and mammals, that live practically under our very noses. Even in the largest of cities it is likely that animals such as foxes are living nearby. If you haven't seen them, it doesn't mean that they are not there, more that they have ways of keeping out of our way and adapting to the urban situation.

Taking trips to sacred sites, showing one's respect, and tuning in with the energies that you experience there is something that I also find most empowering. Ancient sites such as Stonehenge, Avebury and Glastonbury are powerful places, as are the many smaller, lesser known sites that you can discover by studying an ordnance survey map. Old standing stones and stone circles, many of which are rarely used, usually stand on powerful ley lines that were tuned into by our ancestors. Using these sites helps us to develop our sense of feeling, our sense of belonging, an understanding of our ancestors, as well as helping to reinvigorate the complex network of earth energy that flows through them.

Diet is another matter of important consideration. Honouring your physical body by feeding it with a carefully considered diet will help you function better at all levels. Many people on a spiritual path drink plenty of water, avoid sugar and too much salt and eat little or no meat. Choosing organic foods (if your budget can stretch to it) is good for the health of the environment as well as our own and helps to avoid introducing a dreadful mixture of chemicals used in modern farming practices. Fresh raw fruit and vegetables can provide a great deal more vital energy than anything that has been cooked.

Ensuring that we eat breakfast, lunch and dinner and take time to enjoy each, can sometimes be difficult with the hectic pressures of modern life but are important nevertheless. Before I eat I always say a little blessing to myself to thank the Goddess for the bounty the Earth has provided. This needn't be said aloud but to oneself. Taking time to thoroughly chew the food, enjoying every flavour and each aroma helps us to both digest the food properly and appreciate the energy it provides us with.

Addiction to drugs, including alcohol and tobacco, will slow down your progress in self development and these habits need to be addressed at some point if you have them.

Working with local environmental groups, if you have time, can be a worthy occupation. It helps to spread the message to others, as well as putting pressure on the authorities to show more respect. You will find that many witches and other neopagans are involved in such groups. Even if your life doesn't allow time for such ventures, the very least that can be done around the home is to ensure you reduce waste wherever possible, reuse it wherever you can, and in the last resort, ensure that you recycle what remains. All but the most remote parts of Britain have reasonable recycling schemes these days. Some local authorities even collect waste for recycling from your door these days. Working with local community groups can also be very rewarding and help to improve facilities for yourself and those who live around you.

Having said all of this, one vital thing to remember is that everything you do needs to be incorporated into your daily life. It should not significantly affect your working life, the time you spend with friends and family or with your partner. It needs to be thoroughly incorporated into your daily routine – your work, rest and play – without disrupting it. As your head begins to experience the joy of flying in the clouds and fully living in tune with your spiritual higher consciousness, your feet need to remain firmly on the ground!

WHAT ARE THE AIMS OF SELF-DEVELOPMENT?

One metaphor that I particularly like, and probably one more easily appreciated by men, is taken from one of the greatest surviving Celtic texts, the *Mabinogion*[13]. In the story of Peredur (aka Percival) Son of Evrawg, Peredur is reporting back to King Arthur having failed to ask the correct questions on his trip that would have revealed the secrets of the grail. A black, curly-haired woman riding a yellow mule comes along and taunts Peredur for failing in his quest and then says, 'I know where he who wishes the greatest honour and glory can win it: there is a castle on a high mountain, and a girl inside, and the castle is besieged. Whoever lifts that siege will win the greatest fame there has ever been.' Self development is all about examining oneself psychologically, finding out what in this life (and often in previous lives) has created blockages to living totally in tune with the natural energies – with the gods – and gradually removing those blockages. It is about finding balance within. About recognising and balancing the masculine and feminine that resides in all of us and opening oneself up to the higher self and through that connecting to the collective soul consciousness that strives to perfect itself through experience. It is about recognising the value of doing this, whilst recognising that each and every one of us is but a tiny element within the whole vast machinery of collective consciousness and yet each an element of vital importance. If one reaches a certain stage within that development one can choose to serve the gods through one's own spiritual higher consciousness by becoming a conduit between the worlds and an instrument to be used for the greater good as a magician.

To work magic one needs to raise one's consciousness to appreciate and understand the powers and forces behind the physical forms, to develop a spiritual awareness of the 'divine plan', and be prepared to make an individual contribution towards the success of that plan, as best one can, to making that plan.

Imagination, far from being mere fantasy, can become a portal to divine revelation. Witchcraft is just one of several paths that can lead to this ultimate objective. To become an initiate on this path (and this goes for many other paths too) one is stepping into an entirely new relationship between oneself and the rest of creation – a step not to be taken lightly. To become a witch and a magician one needs to be prepared to become an instrument of the gods, undertaking their work by benefiting others by using whatever skills that have been developed throughout one's lives. The path demands a love of life and of the spiritual plane

---

[13] *The Mabinogion* as translated by Jeffrey Gantz.

that animates life alongside an unselfish drive to give and share with others the benefit of one's practical abilities and experience.

Learn to trust the wisdom that comes to you through 'another way of knowing' in the broad multidimensional reality that you had not previously consciously experienced. However, also be prepared that this revelation can bring great changes to your life and that releasing the negativity can often be extraordinarily painful on an emotional level. You need to be prepared to face these challenges and welcome them as part of the learning process. If you find dark negative aspects hidden away deep inside you and fail to deal with them as they surface you run the risk of experiencing a long bout of depression. Development through the various stages of initiation can be a painful, though ultimately worthwhile, process. Spiritual development, getting in touch with the spiritual higher consciousness, inevitably causes what is known in esoteric psychology as a 'Crisis of Evocation' – which is discussed later in more detail.

Using magic we connect with the divine source and allow it to fill us with its energy, to transform us and, if used properly, make us wise. These energies can be used by others for all manner of intentions whether they be good or bad, but unless those intentions are informed by the sacred within and are based on a projection of the will alone, it deteriorates into pure selfish ego satisfaction of little value. To be of true service we must be determined to achieve an advanced stage of spiritual development not for personal gain or egotistical satisfaction, but in order to perform that service, guided by wisdom, motivated by unconditional love, and provided without attachment. Without such qualities what is often found instead is not true service but a combination of good intentions and mixed motives often manifesting as an intricate self-deluding glamour or even fanaticism.

I do not claim that modern Wicca is any more valid than any other system or path, and certainly acknowledge that I still have much to learn myself. However, this system is the one that works for me and as such I commend it to you.

GUIDANCE ON FINDING EQUILIBRIUM WITH THE SOUL

It is important that you first recognise that true equilibrium is the basis of the soul, and that you should practise achieving that equilibrium and then maintaining it through everything you do. This is no mean feat and most will have great difficulty at first. It is a little like walking a tightrope. At first we manage a few steps and fall off, but if we persevere we will

44

eventually manage to maintain that balance with increasing ease. This balance is the foundation from where you need to work. It is a balance between all of our emotions and energies (to be discussed more fully in the next chapter on the Elements), as well as the light and dark.

We are born into life to learn lessons and grow. The trials that we experience in life may well be hard, but if we work our way through them and learn from what we experience, learn from the mistakes rather than continually repeating the same ones over and over, then we shall make progress. It is through learning and growing on the physical plane, learning things that we can only experience on this plane, that we gradually strengthen and perfect our soul to a state that it no longer needs to incarnate and moves forward to a higher spiritual state.

As we progress through this life we will come across many people who interact with us in various ways. Some we will help, others we shall befriend and even fall in love with. But there will be times when even our closest friends turn against us. If we remain centred and balanced we may begin to understand and have sympathy with what we consider betrayal. That betrayal may be justified by something that we have done wrong, from which we need to learn and become humble enough to offer sincere apologies, or it may be aimed at us through jealousy or some other form of malice, in which case it is for the perpetrator of that malice to learn. Do not automatically feel that you have failed simply because you have become a target, it may well mean that you have grown to a point that makes another want what you have worked hard for and yet only they can gain by working equally hard. The trick is recognising when this is true and when it is based on false pride and an immodest glamour. Do not allow your growth let you become vain – a common enough trap – wisdom thrives best with modesty. As the saying goes *"He who knows little thinks he knows much; but he who knows much has learned of his own ignorance. See a person wise in self conceit – there is more hope of a fool than of that person."*

Don't be hasty to condemn others. A non-judgemental attitude is one that every witch should endeavour to adopt. It is all too easy to criticise others for the things they do, the way they look and present themselves and the beliefs they have. We all make mistakes in our life, we make many, but we hope that by making mistakes we learn from them. Other people make mistakes too, and they have to learn the lessons themselves. Who can look in the mirror and be absolutely certain, without a shadow of a doubt, that they are perfect in every way? If we were perfect, would we be here on the physical plane? Along with a belief in reincarnation, more of which will be discussed later in this book, comes the belief that we are here to learn lessons and from those lessons we begin to perfect our spiritual soul. If people around us do not behave as we think they should it is most likely that they are learning some very hard lessons, and that means they are moving forward. Those lessons should be welcomed and encouraged if anything, not condemned. This is not to say, however, that it is wrong to feel angry if you have been wronged. If you feel angry then it is unhealthy to hold that anger within yourself, and if you feel the need to vent that anger take a few deep breaths first and ensure that the outlet for the anger is truly deserving. The rule is 'don't be hasty' but there are times when others need to learn that they cannot treat you as a doormat and need to learn from your reaction.

That fear leads to failure is a particularly key point when working with the occult – or the unseen. It is very easy – in fact a natural reaction – to have some fear or apprehensions when dealing with the unknown. This fear puts up strong blocks. If trying to develop one's psychic abilities, trying to commune with one's guide or other spirits and one has the tiniest amount of fear, or even doubt, then a blockage will hinder that development. As we shall discover in the chapter on initiation, the passwords used in the initiation process are 'perfect love and perfect trust'. It is with this attitude one needs to approach the development of one's deep inner self and thus reach deep into the previously unknown world of the Gods and the Mighty Ones.[14] One needs to learn to be humble before the Goddess and God, and to respect the Spirits, honour them with sincerity but do not fear them and certainly never mock them.

Self development involves balancing oneself between the energies that represent the four elements and between light and dark. When working magic we stand in a Circle – more properly a sphere – putting our spirit firmly in the centre between the four elements, the light above and the dark below. This is where we begin to work magic and that is why establishing a firm equilibrium of the forces is so vitally important if we are to be successful in our work.

As part of the effort to find and maintain that equilibrium it is import to look after our astral and spiritual selves as well as our physical. Unless our physical bodies are functioning well, if we don't show respect for the physical functions, we can hardy expect our astral and spiritual functions to work efficiently no matter how much time we spend in prayer or worship.

Whilst we are discovering and developing the ability to tap into once inexperienced energies it is vital that we keep things in perspective and do not get over ambitious with those new-found abilities. As an individual, no matter how well we manage to open the channels through the higher self

---

[14] 'The Mighty Ones' refers to the spirits of the elements of Earth, Air, Fire and Water. See chapter 7 on *The Elements*.

to our guides, helpers and gods, we are still an individual with severe limitations. We can tap into energies to help those around us, to influence others to help themselves, to heal and nurture that which is within our influence, but we are but a tiny atom in the whole universal energy system. We are but a tiny strand on a massive web. We can do what we can for the sake of the Goddess and God, but no matter how hard we wave our magic wand we cannot reshape the universe.

If you are sincere in mind, body and spirit you will serve yourself and the Goddess and God well. Learn to control your thoughts and work with the natural energies that surround you and you shall reap rewards, grow and move forward as will everything that surrounds you. Work in harmony with the divine within and the divine will work for you. Knock on the doors and they will open for you.

7

THE ELEMENTS

Working with the elements is fundamental to using natural energies and thus working magic. Balancing these energies within yourself is an essential part of your self-development. Imbalance between these elements can lead to emotional turmoil within yourself and consequently relationships with family and friends.

It should be noted that it can often appear to somebody who is just setting out on a magical path that they are under some form of psychic attack. This is highly unlikely, though not entirely impossible, for somebody who has only just started their own development. Until one has fully opened oneself up to the energy flow of the universe, the likelihood of another person fully reaching you is not as likely as an imbalance that one has sensed within your own body or even the development of yet unfamiliar psychic abilities of some kind. The best advice is to remain grounded, do not become paranoid and listen to your body and look within first. As one develops it is necessary for the body to integrate its various aspects of the physical body, the emotional, the mind and the higher spiritual aspects of the soul. As elements of this process begin to take hold one can feel quite a little unbalanced due to the new integration which takes getting used to. It is necessary to focus in on these feelings and sensations, though not to be overly concerned by them. The technical term for these sensations in the world of esoteric psychology is the 'Crisis of Evocation'. It is a perfectly normal and expected part of the development process and something, when properly recognised, to be welcomed and worked with. The feelings will almost certainly soon pass. If you are concerned, endeavour to talk to an elder within your Circle (if you have this option). It is one of the great benefits of working Wicca as a group activity that one has others on a similar path to turn to and consult.

If however you are convinced that you are under psychic attack, and not simply becoming a touch paranoid (which is easily achieved as your sensitivity grows) then you will need to undertake a little psychic defence.

It is sadly true that some people, even in Craft circles, do get jealous of others as they see them grow, though such an attitude is hardly worthy of a sound practitioner. To put up a sound defence there are several methods, one of which I shall touch upon here. First of all take a cleansing ritual bath with salt and lavender oil. Cast a circle around yourself and use your visualisation techniques to put yourself inside a giant mirror ball. See any negative energy directed at you being reflected off in all directions by this ball and failing to reach you. Hold this visualisation for as long as you can and come back to it on occasion. Hanging clear quartz crystals in your window, with an associated intent of protection, will also help (as well as provide some wonderful displays of refracted sunlight throughout your personal space).

Balancing the elements within yourself will help ensure long-lasting health of body, mind and spirit. If you detect an imbalance, use the meditation techniques detailed earlier in this book to work with the element to build it up, or work with the opposing element to recreate balance. If you are already familiar with Circle work you will know that Earth is in the North, Air in the East, Fire in the South and Water in the West. Fire is therefore opposite Earth (Earth has female correspondences to Fire's male) and Water is opposite Air (Air is male, Water female).

EARTH

In all forms of pagan magical traditions, element Earth plays a vital part as one of the five elements. It is usually used in conjunction with the other four (Air, Fire, Water and Spirit) with major magical acts and rituals. Earth generally corresponds with the North and therefore is represented at the Northern point in a magic circle from where that elemental spirit is invoked.

Earth is one of two elements that correspond with the feminine (the other being Water) and thus is passive. Its ritual tool is the Pentagram. Its symbol is an equilateral triangle, with its point downwards and a horizontal line passing through the centre.

In Wiccan magic, Earth tends to correspond with the colour green; therefore a green candle is usually used to mark the Northern quarter of a circle. The Celts, however, correspond elemental Earth with the season of winter and the time of midnight and therefore with the colour black.

The element of Earth corresponds with the physical plane. It is the element to work with regarding earthly matters regarding physical work, career, financial matters and knowledge.

In the physical plane the elementals take the form of gnomes or goblins. Ghob is King of the gnomes (which is where the word 'goblin' comes from) and therefore when invoking the elemental Earth one can call upon Ghob. The word 'gnome' is derived from the Greek word 'gnoma' meaning knowledge. Being earthly creatures, the gnomes correspond with ritual salt, gemstones and rocks. They are durable, stable creatures corresponding with responsibility and thoroughness as positive attributes though also with inflexibility and stubbornness. From Ghob, the King of the gnomes, comes Goibniu in Celtic myth. In the associated myth, Goibniu is a smith-god involved in making highly powerful weapons. He corresponds with healing energies and building abilities. He was eventually Christianised as 'Gobban the Joiner', builder of churches.

You may, at this stage, have a problem with recognising or corresponding the elemental Earth energies with gnomes or goblins. It is all too easy to dismiss such characters as spurious childish fairytale figures. All I can say is that this shouldn't put you off, all will become clear in time. Visualisation is an important element in magic and whilst the Earth elements need not have shape or form under everyday circumstances, it is sometimes necessary for our sub-consciousness (that works in images) to have a form recognisable to us that reinforces the correspondences. Eventually you may find that everything clicks into place. Things that seem strange and spurious at first often end up making sense once a strict meditation regime is established.

EARTH INCENSE

Half a teaspoon of dried alfalfa leaves
One teaspoon of dried pine wood
Four drops of patchouli oil
One pinch of sea salt

First mix the salt and patchouli oil in pestle and mortar, then add the other ingredients and grind.

There are a number of trees and herbs that also correspond to the element Earth. These are: alfalfa; bayberry; barley; blackthorn; briony; buckwheat; fir; fumitory; honeysuckle; hollyhock; myrrh; patchouli; primrose; rhubarb; sage; vervain; tansy; pine; sorrel; strawberry; elm; and clover. You may find it helpful, when working with the element, to use an incense made from some of these herbs. You will find that this helps to strengthen the magical work. For this reason I have included here a recipe for making your own incense which can be burnt on blocks of charcoal in a suitable burner. You will find that a good quality pestle and mortar comes in very useful when making incenses. Whilst gathering you own ingredients is always best (and a wonderful discipline as part of reconnecting with nature is learning about herbs, recognising them, and finding out where and when they grow) health food shops often keep a stock of many dried herbs and oils, or you may even be lucky enough to live near a herbal specialist. Drinking herbal teas is also aid in working with the elements, although be sure to make yourself aware of which ones are unpalatable – or worse – poisonous!

There are also a number of minerals and crystals that correspond to Earth. These are: agate (green and moss); aventurine; coal; emerald; jasper; jet; malachite; marble; obsidian; onyx; peridot; quartz (smoky); salt; tourmaline (black); and turquoise. Again, you will find that these minerals and/or crystals will bring energy to magical work and meditations.

The three astrological birth signs that correspond to Earth are Taurus, Virgo and Capricorn. People born under an Earth sign are likely to be practical and cautious, solid and trustworthy.

Taureans require and exude stability and security throughout their lives. They will rarely take risks, and if they do it will only be after a great deal of thought and when absolutely essential. Taureans are generally practical people, trustworthy and pleasant. Negative aspects include a tendency to be possessive and over-cautious which can lead to them being unenterprising and seem to some rather boring.

Virgoans are often hard and meticulous, precise workers. Although they tend to be intelligent, they often steer clear of taking a leading role as they have a tendency to worry. On the negative side, they tend to avoid getting too close to others which can be perceived as unfriendly or inhospitable.

Capricorns, like all the Earth sign people, also tend to be practical. They often possess a good sense of humour and although they are ambitious they are also caring. Like Taureans they tend to be cautious, especially in personal relationships, though they make good partners. Capricorns are good at work that requires organisational skills and routine. They can become mean and appear stern with their cautious tendency turning into selfishness.

AIR

Air is an element we also take for granted and in modern times have abused considerably. Finding a place where one can breathe pure clean air that is not polluted with toxic chemicals belched out from cars and factories, etc. is sadly impossible these days.

In magical use, the element of air corresponds to the East. It is one of the two elements that are associated with the masculine (the other being fire). Its ritual tool is the athame and/or sword[15] although in some traditions it is the wand. Its symbol is an equilateral triangle, with its point upwards and a horizontal line passing through the centre.

In Wiccan magic, Air corresponds with the colour yellow; therefore a yellow candle is usually used to mark the Eastern quarter of a circle. The Celts, however, correspond elemental Air with the season of spring and the sunrise and therefore with the colour red.

The element of Air corresponds with the mental plane. It is the element to work with regarding the thought process, rationality and intelligence. In the physical plane the elementals take the form of sylphs, nature spirits or fairies. Paralda is King of the sylphs and therefore when invoking the elemental Earth one can call upon Paralda if one chooses. Air can be a difficult element for many to work with especially for those sensual individuals who associate particularly with its elemental opposite of water. The Christian devil is sometimes called the Prince of the Powers of Air and whilst we often take air for granted it deserves at least as much respect as the other elements. Air corresponds with incense, sound and breath. Sylphs are frivolous creatures who appreciate those with rational minds and who think for themselves and detest those who move with the crowd. The negative aspects of air include frivolity, inattention, bragging, arguments and all forms of storms such as tornadoes and hurricanes.

AIR INCENSE

2 teaspoons benzoin gum
1 teaspoon lavender flowers
1 teaspoon cedar wood
$\frac{1}{2}$ teaspoon mint leaves

Mix together in pestle and mortar and grind.

Minerals and crystals that are associated with Air include: amethyst; citrine; emerald; flourite; jade; jasper (mottled); lapis lazuli; moonstone, topaz (yellow) and turquoise. You will find that these minerals and/or crystals will bring energy to magical work and meditations.

The three astrological signs that correspond with Air are Gemini, Libra and Aquarius. People born under an Air sign generally tend to be logical, intelligent and good communicators.

---

[15] The sword or athame penetrates, pierces and cuts through which is why it is associated with the rational mind and therefore the element of Air, at least to those who follow a Celtic inspired path. In Irish Celtic mythology, Air is represented by a spear – one of the Gifts of Faery.

Geminis tend to be versatile and good with money. They can be lively and intelligent though sometimes this can be tempered by a nervous energy and inconsistency. They tend to be logical and ordered and seek variety in both their home life and at work. They make good communicators, are creative but sometimes with a tendency to be over-critical.

Librans can have an obsession with finding balance and as such often find themselves sitting in the middle and being indecisive. They tend to be easy going and diplomatic and often prefer quiet surroundings at home or work. Librans are often romantics in relationships, kind and good with children.

Aquarians tend to be independent types who like to do things by their own rules. They can be stubborn and because of that rarely lose hope in any undertaking. They tend to be highly creative and inventive, friendly, though not necessarily totally reliable. As with other Air signs they make good communicators.

FIRE

Fire is an element that particularly demands respect. As it burns it destroys but also cleanses and makes way for renewal.

In magical use, the element of Fire corresponds to the South. It is one of the two elements that are associated with the masculine (the other being air). Its ritual tool is the wand. Its symbol is a plain equilateral triangle, with its point upwards.

In Wiccan magic, Fire corresponds with the colour red; therefore a red candle is usually used to mark the Southern quarter of a circle. The Celts, however, correspond elemental Fire with the season of summer and the midday sun and therefore with the colour brilliant white.

The element of Fire corresponds with the spiritual plane. It is the element to work with regarding intuition, courage and will. In the physical plane the elementals take the form of sun beams, salamanders or fire dragons. Djin (pronounced dee-yin) is ruler of the salamanders and therefore when invoking the elemental Fire one can call upon Djin if one chooses. Using candles to work magic brings the force of this element into use. There are many positive associations with Fire which include enthusiasm, courage, loyalty, will power, leadership, action and spirituality. Negative associations include hate, jealousy, vindictiveness, ego, conflicts of all kinds and the destructive force of volcanoes. Fire corresponds with candles and oils. Salamanders are active ethereal creatures who will help you achieve your goals as well as giving you protective strength.

FIRE INCENSE

2 teaspoons frankincense
$\frac{1}{2}$ teaspoon oak bark
3 drops of rosemary oil

Put frankincense and oak bark in pestle and mortar and grind. Add rosemary oil.

Minerals and crystals that are associated with Fire include: agate (red); amber; bloodstone; carnelian; diamond; garnet; haematite; iron; jasper (red); ruby; sulphur; and tiger's eye. You will find that these minerals and/or crystals will bring energy to magical work and meditations.

The three astrological signs that correspond with Fire are Aries, Leo and Sagittarius. People born under a Fire sign generally tend to be keen and enthusiastic, sometimes overpoweringly so.

Arians are typified by their courage and enthusiasm, initiative and enterprise. When faced with a challenge they tend to accept it and rush in without heeding the consequences first. Their impulsiveness can often cause them problems because of this. They are likely to have passionate relationships and work with a strong partner.

Leos tend to be generous, proud and creative, but need to keep themselves in check to avoid becoming overbearing. They are generally good, confident and energetic organisers. On the negative side they can have a strong temper. Their urge to lead at all times can make them domineering and arrogant. They can be over-sensitive to criticism.

Sagittarians are generally gregarious, friendly and enthusiastic also with a strong desire to face challenges. They are often versatile and intelligent though with a tendency to take risks. Freedom is important to them, which may well inhibit a long-term relationship. They are not usually interested in material gains rather than spiritual ones.

WATER

Water is an element that is easily associated with and makes up the bulk of our bodies and that of other living creatures.

In magical use, the element of Water corresponds to the West. It is one of the two elements that are associated with the feminine (the other being Earth). Its ritual tool is the chalice. Its symbol is a simple equilateral triangle, with its point downwards.

In Wiccan magic, Water corresponds with the colour blue; therefore a blue candle is usually used to mark the Western quarter of a circle. The Celts, however, correspond elemental Water with the season of autumn and the evening and therefore with the colour grey.

The element of Water corresponds with the emotions. It is therefore the element to work with regarding feelings. In the physical plane the elementals take the form of ondines, water spirits or (as one manifestation) mermaids. Ondines work best with those who are comfortable with their emotions. Positive aspects of Water include compassion, conscience, devotion, receptivity and tranquillity. Negative aspects include apathy, depression, laziness and instability.

WATER INCENSE

2 teaspoons myrrh
$\frac{1}{2}$ teaspoon apple wood
$\frac{1}{2}$ teaspoon heather flowers
$\frac{1}{2}$ teaspoon rowan berries
Put in pestle and mortar and grind.

Minerals and crystals that are associated with Water include: Agate (blue lace); Amethyst; Aquamarine; Coral; Jade; Lapis Lazuli; Moonstone; Mother of Pearl; Pearl; Sapphire; Silver; Sodalite; and Sugalite. You will find that these minerals and/or crystals will bring energy to magical work and meditations.

The three astrological signs that correspond with Water are Cancer, Scorpio and Pisces. People born under a Water sign generally tend to be sensitive, intuitive, emotional and protective.

Cancerians tend to have a protective nature which can be both positive and negative in nature. They are often tempered by a stubborn and sometimes moody streak. Their intuition is generally quite strong and their instinctive decisions are often reliable. Their hard outer shell can hide a soft interior that can easily be hurt.

Scorpions can display quite a mix of difficult behaviour. They can be extremely determined and strong-willed, though sometimes obsessive and arrogant. They can become exceptionally committed to a person or ideal, but can become over melodramatic. Logic tends to suffer when emotions are involved. Whilst they tend to have a strong sense of fair-play and reason, they are not beyond sacrificing friendships if they stand in their way.

Pisceans tend to be sensitive, sympathetic and caring persons often putting other people first, especially their family. They also have a strong and reliable intuition and are good at understanding the needs of those around them. They can be idealistic, though can sometimes be unwilling to make decisions, preferring to let others take the lead for them. They need to ensure that their lack of a strong will does not lead them into becoming exploited.

WATER EXERCISE

Water is especially useful for impregnating ideas or emotions. It is most receptive just above freezing temperature and least receptive at body temperature.

> Fill a bowl or basin with cold water. Use two–three drops of appropriate essential oil if available.
> Magnetise the water with an idea then, as you wash your hands, imagine washing all the uncleanliness from your soul.
> The *'magnetic–astral attractive force'* will draw all weakness from the soul.
> Wash to absorb the idea.

DRAINING AWAY NEGATIVITY

Use a smoky quartz crystal and holding it your right hand, meditate upon any negative emotions that you may have in your mind. Visualise these emotions flowing into the smoky quartz crystal. When you feel you have dumped as much negativity as you can, take the crystal to a tap, or another source of running water, and hold the crystal under it. Keep turning the crystal and visualise the negativity been washed away down the drain until you sense that the crystal has been thoroughly cleansed.

THE PENTAGRAM AND THE HEXAGRAM

The pentagram is a five-pointed star that represents the microcosm of all that is within us all. The five points of the star represent the four elements of Earth, Air, Fire and Water with Spirit as the fifth element dominating at the top. It represents the interconnectedness and interdependence of those five elements.

▲ *Figure 2 – The Pentagram*

The pentagram is the symbol of the magician as a person who can fully understand and use the symbol of the pentagram, can work magic as they recognise and can utilise the elements of nature in balance with and mastered by the spirit. This ability is within all of us, therefore it is known as the sign of the microcosm, as it is in the macrocosmic world all around us. The elements of the Universe find equilibrium as they are mastered by the laws of the Universal Spirit. The pentagram, there-fore, wielded by one who works in tune with those universal laws of nature, is one of the most potent symbols that exist.

The pentacle – a pentagram enclosed within a surrounding circle – as found as the centre-piece on a witch's altar[16] is often worn as a silver pendant by witches and other neo-pagans alike representing their beliefs in the interconnectedness and interdependence of the powers of nature and spirit.

▲ *Figure 3 – The 'A' in the Pentagram.*

The word (which has unfortunately become somewhat of a cliché due to its use by conjurers) 'Abracadabra' hides a pentagram as it contains five 'A's which when ranged in a circle (figure 3) form a pentagram. With the five 'A's removed one is left with six consonants that relate to the hexagram. When arranged in diminishing form (figure 4), as in the figure below, it contains thirty (or 3×10) 'A's. The number thirty using roman numerals (two 'X's for tens and two 'V's for fives) can be arranged to form a symbol (figure 5) closely related to the pentagram – the hexagram. The hexagram (figure 6) sometimes referred to the Seal of Solomon. Whereas the pentagram is the symbol of the micro-cosm, the hexagram is the symbol of the macrocosm. To a Jew it is the Star of David.

---

[16] See chapter of the 'Tools of the Craft'.

▲ *Figure 4 – Abracadabra.*

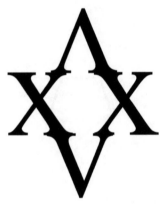

▲ *Figure 5 – The number 30 using roman numerals can represent the hexagram.*

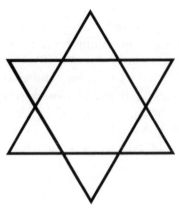

▲ *Figure 6 – The Hexagram.*

The six-pointed star is basically two interlocking triangles, one pointing up and the other pointing down. It represents the ultimate trilogy in duplicate – as above, so below; the macrocosm and the microcosm combined. In other words it symbolises what is seen as manifesting as the God and Goddess in the outside world and that which is replicated within us all.

The hexagram is the combination of the downward pointing triangle given to a witch at the first initiation with the upward pointing triangle given at the third (when one becomes a High Priestess or High Priest). It also incorporates the individual symbols used to represent the elements of Earth, Air, Fire and Water. Thus it is a symbol of completeness.

The hexagram is incorporated into one's robes by tying the cords worn around one's waist with a reef knot.

8

THE OTHER WORLDS

The Celtic myths are full of stories regarding heroes and shamans who entered the 'other world' on a quest for inner truths. They are a race that always had one foot in both worlds and they appear to have had a reasonable understanding of the reincarnation process. It is through the many Celtic allegorical myths that we can discover a great deal of inspiration. Perhaps the best known of these are the Arthurian tales – originally pagan but later Christianised (and therefore somewhat suffering from a confusing overlay) – which still stand out today and are studied by many.

Shamans throughout many cultures of the world used, as many still do, mind-altering drugs to induce a state of expanded consciousness in order to travel across the planes to commune with spirits of all kinds and experience the divine. Druid shamans of the Celtic tribes would have used such techniques before going into battle to summon up spirits to help their own tribe in the days ahead. Witches are believed, as I understand some still do, to have used mushrooms such as fly algeric to enter a state of trance. Fly algeric was one of the ingredients used in the 'flying ointment' of old which is where the idea of witches flying through the sky on broomsticks probably comes from. Other ingredients of flying ointment include belladonna (deadly nightshade) which is also highly poisonous – I would therefore not recommend experimenting with such herbs.

However, it is not necessary to use drugs to reach a state of trance or meditation in order to expand one's consciousness of the other planes of existence.

Our limited senses in the normality that we generally experience pick up a tiny fraction of the light and sound frequencies or vibration rates that exists throughout all of nature. Many other animals seem to experience a much broader range than we do, though it is still comparatively limited, and it is highly likely that we humans also did in the past but have shut down these senses for whatever reason.

Working within these other planes is fundamental to all mystical esoteric traditions. The five senses are perfectly reasonable instruments for experiencing that which exists on the physical plane. However, this does not constitute the whole of existence but merely the exoteric that science can readily confirm by using a microscope, etc. The occultist, which ever path she or he is following, goes further than the scientist and uses the power of the spiritual sense, through the mind, to discover and explore a whole greater reality that exists beyond the physical plane. In the worlds beyond the physical exist the forces that animate and actuate life and its circumstances.

The Celts, as we have already mentioned, had a reasonable understanding of the other planes of existence, of the 'Other world' as they knew it. However, a more detailed understanding can be drawn from the mystical Judaic and eastern religions and it is here I have turned to base my own understanding and explanation. The planes are viewed in many different ways and the way they operate has many descriptions. These differences of opinion spring more from the efforts to try and explain a relatively complex relationship in layman terms than a misunderstanding of the process itself.

The 'Other worlds' or 'Other planes' of existence are often depicted as seven levels, or rather four including the physical with the other three being sub-divided into two each. Beyond these dimensions exists the Great Void from where each dimension originates. These dimensions are known as the physical, lower and upper astral, lower and upper elemental, and lower and upper spiritual.

GREAT VOID
UPPER SPIRITUAL
LOWER SPIRITUAL
UPPER ELEMENTAL
LOWER ELEMENTAL
UPPER ASTRAL
LOWER ASTRAL
PHYSICAL

An alternative and equally common way of forming these planes is as follows:

THE ULTIMATE PLANE
THE DIVINE PLANE
THE SPIRITUAL PLANE
THE MENTAL PLANE
THE ASTRAL PLANE
THE ELEMENTAL PLANE
THE PHYSICAL PLANE

In this pictorial representation, the physical existence enters the astral through the elemental plane. The elemental plane is seen as containing the force and the astral the form. Therefore images begin being generated on the physical, pick up force and form as they 'bubble up' through the elemental planes, continue to some point in the upper planes and then presumably manifest themselves by passing back down through the various planes to return to the physical plane.

Personally I visualise this process in yet a third way. Using the first example I see the two aspects of the upper and lower astral plane as shallow and deep, as they vibrate at a lower rate than the physical. The lower elemental I place above the astral with the physical above that. Above the physical I place the upper elemental plane followed by the two spiritual planes which I see as vibrating at a higher rate than the physical. In my explanation, as one works 'between the worlds', the physical expands outwards both down into the lower vibrations of the astral and lower elemental planes (the astral containing the force and the lower elemental containing the elements of form of earth, air, fire and water) and upwards into the upper elemental (containing the fifth element of human spirit) and the higher dimensions of the spiritual planes themselves. Thus one is working with the elementals through visualisation directly to put one's thought forms into force in the physical, whilst at the same time working with other spiritual entities from the spiritual planes through one's own elemental spirit. One is thus working in partnership with the spiritual entities, using one's own abilities to utilise the elements whilst at the same time asking your own spiritual helpers for their efforts to build on yours. This, of course, requires one to have built up this relationship with the spiritual plane in order to work in tune and harmony with one's feet firmly planted throughout each plane of existence.

During Circle work and meditational visualisation work, one expands from the physical broadening one's vibrational contact both up and down before stepping out back into the physical and drawing what has been created towards you.

This then is how I might represent my version of the seven planes on paper:

DEEP SPIRITUAL PLANE
LESSER SPIRITUAL PLANE
UPPER ELEMENTAL PLANE (Human Spirit)
PHYSICAL PLANE
LOWER ELEMENTAL PLANE (Earth, Air, Fire and Water)
LESSER ASTRAL
DEEP ASTRAL

The other planes do not adhere to the commonly accepted rules, as we experience them, of time and space. This is where the occult meets metaphysical science. Whilst they are depicted as different levels they in fact coexist all around us. The physical as we experience it, can be regarded as little more than an illusion (or 'maya'). Every physical object, ourselves included, consists of a group of constantly shifting atoms, moving at varying rates. Each atom consists of three elements that take up a fraction of the 'space' that actually exists. The other dimensions exist between these spaces and vibrate at a rate not normally experienced in our waking lives except by certain individuals who are either born or become sensitive to these levels of vibration.

It is by looking between the spaces of the physical that we previously accepted as all that is solid and real that we discover a whole new reality that is deeper and broader than we could ever have imagined.

This concept, for me, fits in with the Celtic world view of the underworld and over-world, as well as the concept found in many eastern traditions. It also fits in well with the model provided by the Kabbalist's Tree of Life. However, it is only a model. The boundaries between the various planes are not so clear cut and do not fit so neatly into little boxes on which we can put a label.

The dimensions represent all that can be experienced by the complete human being. Many, however, are only vaguely aware of, or accept, much more than what they experience on the physical plane during their waking hours even though they enter the lower astral dimensions during times of sleep. The upper dimensions, the upper elemental and spiritual planes, contain the immortal elements of a human being – the complete soul which stays with us through all incarnations. It is through this area that we are able, with work, to access past life memories and a whole range of knowledge that can be put to good use for ourselves, for others, and for the benefit of the spirits with whom we share this greater reality. The individuality is bisexual in as much as it contains the creative male and female element. Future incarnations and past lives can therefore be either masculine or feminine. In fact, it is almost certain that each soul will incarnate in a number of male and female lives in order to fully experience the karmic 'bank-balance' of both light and dark factors.

The lower dimensions contain that which makes up the current personality and is not fully taken with us although part of the personality moves up the plane on death to become part of the Higher Self. It is because the Physical plane resides between the higher and lower planes that we are able to fully experience all of existence and why it is necessary for us to incarnate in the Physical plane in order to grow. Once we move into the Higher planes we no longer have access to the Lower planes and therefore our ability to learn from that experience is limited.

REINCARNATION

There is a commonly accepted understanding throughout witchcraft, as there are in other traditions including parts of the Christian church[17], of the process of reincarnation[18]. The soul resides outside of our bodies in the other world where it is not able to fully grow and expand without experience in the physical plane. It therefore reincarnates many times in order to gradually experience all that the physical plane has to offer until it reaches the stage of spiritual development where it no longer needs to reincarnate and moves on to take on a greater spiritual role. The soul has by this time become what some traditions would call an 'ascended master' or 'inner plane adepti'.

Once a soul has fully withdrawn from the physical plane – and some take their time to withdraw for various reasons – the individual elements of the soul re-enter what Wiccans call the Summerland. Here it is fully reconnected with all mortal memories and has contact with other souls within a group situation. It is here that the soul is able to assess the life it has just had, the lessons learnt from it and the lessons learned from previous lives, discuss matters with its guides and others within its own group who would be around the same level of development. It is then able to judge what other lessons may or may not be needed to learn with the benefit of the objectivity offered by the spiritual plane. The soul can only learn such lessons, and thus grow, on the physical plane, as it is only on the physical plane that it can venture into each of the seven planes.

If the soul is to reincarnate, the raw materials needed for the next personality are gathered together before it ensouls a foetus sometime between the moment of conception and birth.

There are many different forms of souls, or spirits, that can be identified and found through the Otherworld. There are those we have already mentioned – the souls that are still in the reincarnation process and those that have grown beyond this stage (the inner plane adept) – but there are also spirits that have never entered the reincarnations process as well as elemental spirits of various descriptions, some of which have already been mentioned in the chapter *The Elements*. Some of the spirits that have never entered the incarnation process are what some people would call 'angels'. One can also access one's own soul group to which is attached a guide, or guardian. We all have a guide, whether we are consciously aware of them or not.

---

[17] Though generally elements of the Christian church on the fringe such as the spiritualists.
[18] Not officially abolished by the Roman Church until the 6th Century.

64

It is possible to make contact with all sorts of spirits, your own guide probably being the easiest as he or she is likely to be the most willing. Many people have psychic 'gifts' of one sort or another.

There are generally three ways of experiencing psychic contact – through hearing (clairaudient); seeing (clairvoyant); and feeling (clairsentient). Some people experience these abilities with barely any effort at all, in fact in some cases the ability comes as quite an unwelcome shock to those who do not understand what is going on, but whether we find it easy or have to work hard at developing psychic ability, I am convinced that we all have the ability in us.

A spiritualist, or those who follow the Spiritualist Church, tend to contact the spirits, or souls, of those who have been incarnate and have passed on, probably to reincarnate again. This can be quite interesting, though it should be remembered that these spirits are not necessarily highly developed and may well play all sorts of games. For anyone familiar with Internet chat rooms I would suggest that communicating with these spirits is a little like this sort of communication. You may well find a spirit who will give you a straight forward chat, you may equally well find one that is hiding behind a mask and will play games. When working magic, we tend to avoid contact with that level of spirit, as will be discussed in the final chapter of this book. Magicians tend to work with their own guides, elementals and the higher developed spirits or 'inner plane adepti' and, most importantly, one's own higher consciousness or soul.

MYTH OF THE DESCENT OF THE GODDESS INTO THE UNDERWORLD

One of the better known Celtic texts, and one that appears to have its source in Eygptian myth, is that of the descent of the Goddess into the Underworld. It is an analogy that includes a reference to the seven planes of existence, that also relate to the seven degrees of development, and the concept of reincarnation. This is an adaptation of the myth as told by the modern Wiccan scholar Raven Grimrassi as well as by Stewart and Janet Farrar.

The Goddess endeavoured to solve all the mysteries, even the mystery of Death so she journeyed to the Underworld in her boat, on the Sacred River of Descent. She soon came before the first of seven gates to the Underworld. The Guardian challenged her, demanding one of her garments for passage, for nothing may be received except that something is given in return. At each of the gates the Goddess was required to pay the price of passage. The Guardians told her that she must strip off her garments and set aside her jewels as nothing may be taken into the Underworld.

The Goddess surrendered her jewels and her clothing to the Guardians. At the first gate she surrendered her sceptre, at the second her crown, at the third her necklace, at the fourth her ring, at the fifth her girdle, at the sixth her sandals, and at the seventh her gown. The Goddess eventually stood naked and was presented thus to the Lord of the Underworld.

Her beauty was such that he himself knelt as she entered. He laid his crown and his sword at her feet and said: 'Blessed be your feet that have brought you to this place.' Then he rose and said to the Goddess: 'Stay with me I pray, and receive my touch upon your heart.'

The Goddess replied to the Lord of the Underworld: 'But I love you not because you cause all the things that I love, and delight in, to fade and die.'

'My Lady,' replied the Dark Lord, 'It is age and fate against which you speak. I am helpless, for age causes all things to wither, but when men die at the end of their time, I give them rest, peace and strength. For a time they dwell with me alongside fellow spirits; they may then return to the realm of the living. But you are so lovely, and I ask you not to return, but abide with me here.'

But she answered: 'No for I do not love you.' Then the Lord said: 'if you refuse to embrace me, then you must kneel to death'. The Goddess answered him: 'If it is to be then it is fate!' So she knelt in submission before the hand of Death, and he scourged her with so tender a hand that she cried out: 'I know your pain, and the pain of love.'

The Dark Lord raised her to her feet and said: 'Blessed are you my Queen and my Lady.' Then he gave to her the five kisses of initiation, saying: 'Only thus may you attain knowledge and joy.'

He taught her all of his mysteries, and he gave her the necklace which is the cycle of rebirth. She taught him her mysteries of the sacred chalice which is the cauldron of rebirth. They loved and joined in union with each other, and for a time the Goddess dwelled in the realm of the Dark Lord.

There are three mysteries in the life on Man which are: Sex, Birth and Death (love controls them all). To fulfil love, you must return again at the same time and place as those who loved before. And you must meet, recognise, remember and love them again. But to be reborn you must die and be made ready for a new body. To die you must be born, but without love you may not be born amongst your own.

Our Goddess is inclined to favour love, joy and happiness. She guards and cherishes her hidden children in this life and the next. In death she reveals the way to her communion, and in life she teaches them the magic of the mystery of the Circle (which is set between the worlds of the men and gods).

This myth can be viewed in different ways. On one hand it describes the mystery of the cycle of birth, life, death and rebirth and how the Lord and Lady came to work together in order to make this possible. It analogises the passage to the underworld – or otherworld – through the seven gates and what needs to be done in order to achieve contact. It also corresponds to the seven levels of development for a soul on the physical plane, the seventh being reached when the final garments of physical existence are finally stripped away.

Many people who discover magic seem to think that it can be used to embellish oneself with materialistic wealth and can be used to manipulate people into love, or worse. This myth, however, teaches us that to reach the heady heights of the Otherworld we need to strip ourselves of many things. We need to strip ourselves of our ego, our self-importance, our materialistic fetishes, the false façade that we put up for the benefit of others, the reliance on the standing we have amongst our peers and the value we put on our accomplishments. When we are able to strip ourselves of all these things, and it isn't as easy as it sounds, then we are able to present ourselves as our true unadorned self – our spirit. This is the meaning given to the Goddess who relinquishes her sceptre, her crown, her, girdle, ring, etc. The final thing that she strips off being her robe, an analogy for our physical body – that shell that we rely on in this plane.

9

AN ALTAR AT HOME

An excellent way to help reconnecting with the elements, and to provide a readily available focus for your spirituality, is to build yourself a permanent altar in a quiet corner of your home. The altar becomes a daily reminder of your connection with the gods, becomes a place to sit and meditate and, if and when you feel ready, as a place to work magic. Keep it, and treat it, with respect. It is a sacred place and needs to be regarded as such. It needn't, however, be a static never changing altar. In fact it should be in a constant state of change and transformation as the Wheel of the Year turns and the seasons change. Use different colour altar cloths for the different seasons – this will help remind the subconscious and conscious mind of the Wheel of the Year – and decorate it with seasonal flowers or other items that remind you of the place in the year's cycle. As much as anything else, it helps to keep your altar looking beautiful as well providing a source of natural energy.

As with all things pagan there are no hard and fast rules. What feels right and what comes naturally to you is always best. If someone tells you that you *must* do something a certain way then simply ignore them. Advice is good and useful if you need it and actively seek it, otherwise make the judgement yourself and if something feels wrong, simply don't do it, or change it. Dogma has no place in this path.

Your own personal altar at home is an excellent way to help you reconnect with Nature. On it you can keep a permanent reminder of the elements, keep seasonal flowers, rocks that you have collected in a favourite spot, in fact anything that takes your fancy. If it appeals to you then it can become a wonderful place to sit or stand and meditate, or simply ponder for a few quiet moments.

To start building your altar, find yourself an old wooden table, or make yourself something from part of an old tree trunk[19]. Cover it in

---

[19] Avoid metal and plastic. Spirits do not respond well to the presence of iron or steel, and plastics do not conduct natural energies.

▲ *The altar.*

a cloth. You may like to hunt around fabric shops for something that appeals to you or make something yourself; items always have that much more meaning and energy if you have put some personal effort into them yourself. If you feel particularly creative, decorating the cloth with some appropriate embroidery designs can make it look even nicer and add even more of your own magnetic energy. Alternatively you may already have a suitable piece of cloth or other material. Something that has been in the family for a while would be good.

Traditionally the element Earth would be represented by a pentagram painted, carved or burnt into a flat, circular piece of copper or hardwood. The pentagram – a five pointed star within a circle – represents the microcosm of Earth. The five points on the star represent the elements of Earth, Air, Fire and Water, with the fifth point (the top one) representing the elemental spirit.

The pentagram, once placed on the altar, can become a place where you leave offerings of flowers, seeds, stones, etc. and is also used as a focus for charging items such as oils, crystals and talismen.

If, however, you don't feel the need for a proper pentagram, something else that represents the element earth to you would be appropriate. Maybe some rocks, crystals, or simply a living plant in a pot full of earth.

Salt is also often found on an altar which also represents Earth and can used for mixing in the water for cleansing purposes.

For the element of Air it is usual to introduce something like an incense using a censer, a jos-stick or essential oil. Keep a little incense on the altar. Again the choice of incense is your own, but you could use a flavour that is appropriate to the season – maybe a flowery one such as patchouli or lavender in summer, and a woody one such as sandalwood in autumn. You could use an oil burner or if you are not keen or are sensitive to strong smells then just a little oil dropped on to the surface of water would suffice. Incense tends to help stimulate the senses and is regularly used in meditation and occult work. Alternatively you could use something else like flowers or a feather.

For the element of Fire it is traditional to use candles. It is hard to imagine a witch not working with candles. Much work is done by candle-light as it not only provides representation of the element Fire, but also a natural light without the unwelcome energy presented by electricity.

Witches and other pagans often use three candles on the altar. One placed centrally on the altar represents the 'One Source' and is usually symbolically lit first. It also represents the burning spirit within us all. The other two, placed on the left and right hand sides of the altar, represent the Goddess and the God (Goddess on left). The candle-sticks used for these are often chosen so that they symbolically represent the Goddess and God in design. Most often the Goddess is symbolised by a representation of the Moon, the God by a representation of the Sun[20]. When lit, the Goddess and God candles are lit from the central altar candle representing their manifestation from the One Source.

The colours used for the Goddess and God candles are a matter of personal preference, as with most things. One could use a silver candle for the Goddess and a gold one for the God (moon and sun); alternatively a green candle for the Goddess and a red one for the God (Venus and Mars, masculine and feminine); a black candle for the Goddess and white for the God (representing the two polarities and the pillars between which one stands to work magic); or simply two white candles. The choice may depend on your personal preferences, or what you have available at the time.

Water is an easy element to incorporate on the altar. A small bowl (pick one that is attractive to you or has some spiritual symbolism on it) to contain the water is sufficient. It is best not to use tap water as it generally contains all sorts of chemicals. Natural spring water is best – and if you are able to collect it yourself from a special place then all the better.

Once you have decided what you fancy, found a nice quiet place to keep your altar, away from interference by others, try to keep it a sacred area. It's a good idea to ask anyone you live with to respect that little bit of space as your own, and not to touch it or leave items on it. It's nice to use this space to keep seasonal flowers so that it is in tune with the ever turning wheel of the year. In spring it is nice to bring some colour to

---

[20] Paired sets of this design of candle-stick seem to be readily available.

your altar with some daffodils from the garden, or if you don't have a garden you could buy some from a shop. At Yule it would be traditional to decorate the altar with sprigs of holly and/or mistletoe.

The altar, as I have said, is a good place to sit and quieten down or meditate, especially at the end of a hectic day when getting ready for bed. Whilst at home I like to start the day off by standing before my altar, saying a short blessing to myself and lighting a candle. For safety's sake I snuff out the candle before going out or going to bed.

It is normal to consecrate an altar candle before it is placed in its holder. To do this take some oil (I use a mixture of olive oil, lavender and rosemary) and put a little on the candle. Using your hand work the oil up the candle in a clockwise spiral fashion saying something like . . .

"I consecrate this candle in the names of the Lady and Lord, Goddess and God."

Don't just *say* the words, do it with reverence and feeling. Put some passion into your work and you will find it so much more rewarding.

10

MEDITATION (PART TWO)

Having become well practised in the basic meditation and visualisation techniques, and having built up a reasonable personal understanding of the elements and the Otherworld, it is then time to start looking a bit deeper at what is actually happening whilst in a meditational state.

We have already discussed what is happening to the level of brain activity and how during a meditational state these patterns move from the beta state into the alpha. What we need to consider now is the actual route that our energy is being taken on the physical level so that we can more fully understand what is happening when we start moving beyond the physical. There is a gland positioned in the lower centre of the brain, roughly between one's eyebrows and an inch or so inside, known as the pineal gland. This is the gland that many traditions recognise as the 'third eye'.

Scientists have yet to fully understand what this gland does, although one of its functions is clearly to regulate some of our hormonal levels. Esotericists on the other hand are aware that it is the gateway through which we are able to access the energy vibrations of the other planes of existence – the 'Otherworlds'. A scientist most likely, for lack of physical evidence, would determine that the effects of deep meditation and trance are entirely psychological. A large part of the methods used are certainly psychological, and there is certainly a considerable psychological benefit to be gained from the process, but psychology is only a tool used to the deeper realities rather than the end in itself. To the regular practitioner the experience becomes very real indeed. Just because there is no directly measurable and scientifically indisputable evidence that what is being experienced beyond the physical plane is real, this in itself does not make it any less real. It is a problem for science to accept more than the esotericist. It is primarily a matter of acceptance and faith in oneself that what is being experienced is more than fantasy, fantastic as it is, and once the deeper reality is accepted then evidence of the work done on the astral, elemental and spiritual planes becomes clear to the practitioner, even if not entirely provable to the scientist. This is one area where metaphysics moves outside of the generally acceptable arena of mainstream science, although the gulf between the two is gradually coming together for the eventual benefit of all.

Whilst meditating, recognise that it is the pineal gland that you are focusing on, though it is important not to concentrate too hard. It is not only one's own subconscious that is being contacted. Through the third eye we are able to draw in energies from nature – from outside – as well as focusing on energies from within. It is with the benefit of this gland that we are able to focus on the auras of living things, to feel the previously invisible, unseen (i.e. 'occult') energies from nature, and from there, to connect with the spirit world as we discussed earlier in this book.

Most important of all, however, we will start the process of contacting our own higher consciousness – our spiritual soul – and in doing so we will have started on the process of integrating the physical, emotional and mental elements of our body with the rest of what constitutes the 'whole' self that resides on the spiritual plane.

It would be folly to expect the average person to be able to get results after just a few weeks (or even just a few months) working on self-development and practising meditation as a daily element in that process. Some people have a natural ability and develop quickly, but the average person may require months, or even a few years, of dedication to get the full effect. Unfortunately far too many people expect to be able to learn the theory from reading a few books and then jump in to the deep end and expect to swim like an olympic athlete and, when they find they can't, give up on the whole process and condemn it as impossible. An esoteric path *does* demand faith and dedication. Unless one is prepared to put the work in, one cannot expect to get the rewards and results in return; it's as simple as that.

The techniques discussed earlier in this book, the meditations as well as the chakra balancing, will all help to fully develop the third eye function and energy flows. One thing to remember when trying to focus on the third eye is not to try *too* hard. Do not go into a meditation and put all one's effort into focusing on this part of the brain or it will not work. This is because by putting effort into the focus you are utilising the conscious part of the brain. What you need to do is allow everything to flow naturally, on its own. By all means be aware that you need to focus on the third eye, but let it happen on its own in a very relaxed fashion. Bear in mind also the advice found in the earlier section of this book on the *Guidance on finding equilibrium with the soul*, particularly the notes on entering the unknown with fear or apprehension in one's mind.

What you are doing whilst meditating is perfectly natural. You are indeed making contact with a far greater depth of reality than you have perhaps ever experienced before, but it has always been there whether you were conscious of it or not. There is nothing to be feared, in fact quite the reverse. Being able to reach so far into all of the Otherworld is something to be celebrated and welcomed rather than feared, even if some of the inner truths you find there make you realise how much personal inner work you need to do, albeit to great benefit.

Inside the pineal gland are small crystalline elements. When you have fully tuned into this element of the brain, so neglected by humans over the recent millennia, you are awakening a part of your body that brings a whole new vitality to your entire system. It awakens not just your spiritual element, but affects your physical, emotional and mental elements too. It is this pineal gland, or third eye (as far as I am concerned), that is known in alchemy is the 'alchemical stone' or in Eastern terminology 'the jewel of the yogis'. Once the third eye has been fully awakened it causes changes throughout oneself that eventually leads to a magnificent transmutation if the work is kept up.

Once reasonably adept at focusing on the pineal gland you will discover that you can use it to channel energies in both directions. You can take a crystal, a herb, or anything else, hold it in your receiving hand (the left if right-handed), or hold it up to your forehead, and feel the energies flowing from the item. At first you may just feel the energy as a kind of warm or cold, rapidly vibrating sensation. With practice you will learn to differentiate between the various energies. This is aided by allowing the flow of energy to pass in both directions in a natural and effortless fashion. You will also discover that you can channel (or draw into yourself and focus) natural energies to use in healing and other esoteric work in much the same way, using the energy flowing in to identify the required balancing energies that can then be allowed to flow out.

The exercises that follow should help you take the techniques of meditation discussed earlier in this book and develop them further. However, I would satisfy yourself that you have practised basic meditation and visualisation techniques to the point where you can do them with ease before moving on to these more advanced techniques. It is not that they are in any way dangerous, especially if you fully integrate the grounding exercises described earlier in this book, but you will struggle to fully appreciate the more advanced techniques if you haven't to some degree mastered the basics. It would be a little like trying to drive a high-powered racing car before learning how to drive a normal road vehicle.

ADDRESSING COMPLEXES

Throughout our lives our mental brain is capable of building up all manner of subconscious suggestions that meld together (sometimes in what appear to be most illogical ways) to form what psychologists call complexes. People we interact with (more often parents and siblings during our formative years) often throw suggestions at us, for whatever reason, that our conscious mind cannot accept or assimilate. This could be a situation from our childhood where for some reason one of our parents tells us that we are 'stupid', 'naughty' or 'dirty'. The suggestion can sink into our subconscious and, because we feel it cannot be justified or dealt with in the conscious mind, it lodges itself alongside other thoughts to build up what can seem to be irrational complexes. For instance, other situations where a similar suggestion is thrown at us can link up with the previous suggestion and begin to build into a complex that has no logical justification. These complexes can affect our behaviour and reaction to things in our physical world in unpredictable and unexplainable ways. These complexes are rarely found in isolated units, but part of a chain with all sorts of entangled side issues.

During the process of self-development we start to look objectively at the way we behave and react to certain situations. We may well find that we react to certain situations in a way that we cannot explain or rationalise. It could be that we are not happy that we reacted in a certain way, but that at the time we seemed unable to react any differently.

By entering a meditation, once our mind is steadied and blank, we can then use this as an objective canvas and work back from one of these situations. Look back to whatever it was that seemed to cause the reaction – it could be a word, phrase, or even a particular chain of events. When you have found what appears to have been a key, focus in on this and see what other memories seem to crop up that are associated with it. Don't force the issue, or try to analyse the situation consciously, allow your thoughts to flow on their own as freely as you can. You will find that this process can take you back to unexpected memories, quite often from the distant past (sometimes even from a past life memory). These memories can appear to be quite minor events in our life, but the fact that they are still readily retrievable shows that they have been stored for good reason. It is said, and I believe it to be true, that we remember everything in some form or another, but those memories that do have an effect on us are more easily retrieved than the mundane that have not affected us in any way. You will know when you have found the root as you will most likely experience a sense of sudden realisation. You may even suddenly feel a sense of inner self annoyance that something so simple and obvious (at least obvious now that it has become clear) could have affected you throughout your life. It is important, however, not to be too hard on yourself everyone has such complexes, but forgive yourself and understand that you can now deal with it and feel good that you can.

Bringing that memory from the subconscious into the conscious mind we are then able to deal with it and understand why we reacted how we did. Having done this we are able to start breaking down the complex. Bear in mind that some complexes can have many side shoots and that having dealt with some of the root causes there may well be other aspects that need to be dealt with as well. However, having started the process you will find that you have a greater understanding of yourself, and are able to control your reactions in future in a way that you are much happier with.

This process can dig up some *very* deeply buried emotional memories that have buried themselves in the subconscious because your conscious ego-driven self decided that you are not able to deal with them at the time. Unless dealt with, they sit in our minds, fester and grow in ways that can cause us a great deal of confusion. Having decided to seek the root causes of these complexes, however, we have made a conscious decision that we are ready to take control and integrate our conscious with our sub-consciousness and will therefore be ready to deal with them, even if it does temporarily cause us an emotional reaction.

This integration is all part of the 'Technique of Integration' that eventually leads to fully integrating our physical, emotional and mental elements with our higher consciousness – or spiritual soul.

I have broken down many of these complexes in my own life. In an effort to elaborate I shall give just two examples:

The first is what I considered to be an irrational fear of dogs. It was not a deeply seated fear that caused me to cower in the corner whenever I saw a dog (though I have seen this in some people) but a fear, or at least a deep apprehension. By meditating upon this I went back to a memory from a time when I was around eleven years old. I had been walking down an alleyway close to my mother's house when a dog suddenly started barking very loudly from behind a fence right next to me. The shock caused my body to lurch and freeze in such a way that I was unable to take a breath for quite some time. No matter how hard I tried I could not breathe. This continued up to the point where I thought I was going to pass out. The moment passed, of course, but that memory and fear of not being able to breathe was related to the dog. Meditating further on this matter I went back to what I thought were relatively vague memories from my early childhood. I was at my grandmother's house where there was a terrier. I must have been around eighteen months old as I know that my grandmother had such a dog when I was living at her place with my mother, so it is a very early memory. The dog, in its excitement, knocked me over and I bashed my head causing me pain and a long bout of tears. These two memories were enhanced by other minor incidents as well. By dragging these memories from my subconscious I was able to rationalise the 'fear' and deal with it. Later, I took some time to learn more about dogs and how to master them. I am still not particularly keen on dogs, I am very much a 'cat person', but I no longer have any concerns about dogs, even packs of hunt dogs close to a kill which I have faced during my times in animal rights groups.

The second example had a more profound effect on my life. After splitting up with a girlfriend with whom I lived I realised I hated being alone. A condition that is probably not uncommon. By meditating upon this I was first taken back to the memory that was not buried deeply, but one that has been in my conscious memory for some time. It was the emotional trauma caused when my father suddenly and unexpectedly left my mother when I was fourteen. It was quite a shock for my sister and me, not to mention my mother who was totally distraught. I felt that I had been abandoned and left alone to cope at a very difficult time in my life – going through adolescence and preparing for examinations. Meditating further I was taken back to yet another very early memory of being in a pram. My father had taken me out and left me outside the local public house, presumably so that he could pop in for a quick drink. The memory is not very detailed, but I recall a lot of very strange men leaning over the pram in a crowd and scaring me. I can even recall the smell of stale cigarettes and beer on their breath. They meant no harm, but the fear of being alone is strong. To add to the complex, both these memories involved my father leaving me alone. I was therefore able to not only deal with what I had originally recognised as the fear of being alone, but also with some very negative aspects of my father which I realised affected me greatly, but which I had not previously fully dealt with.

Another similarly associated aspect of this work, at least similar in as much as it relies on us being able to assess ourselves objectively, is to consider our 'glamours'. Glamours can be those false images that we put up to impress others and even to impress our own lower consciousness. We can fool others, and ourselves, into believing that we are something that we are not. It could be an air of confidence that we portray, an identity that we prefer because we have been impressed with a similar one in others, or even an ability that we would like to think we have but have not properly developed because we haven't put in, or been prepared to put in, the necessary work. It may even be our desire to be seen as a witch (as an example) – something that says to others 'hey look! I'm different' – but which in reality is little more than some elaborate jewellery and wishful thing hiding a false façade.

When we gain the ability to be objective about ourselves, being *totally* honest, we might have to admit that in fact we are actually only doing this to impress an idea on ourselves and others for egotistical reasons that in fact serve our higher selves very poorly.

Glamours can also manifest themselves in other ways. They could be, for instance, the glamour of love and being loved or being popular; the glamour (associated with being loved) of personal magnetism; the glamour of always being busy; the glamour of intellect; the glamour of material gain (keeping up with the Joneses); etc. etc. There is a long list of such glamours, but I'm sure you get the idea.

Through considering these 'glamours' during meditation, we can start to analyse ourselves objectively, begin to understand why it is that we feel the need for these glamours, and find a way of breaking them down. It may take hard work, and being this honest with oneself can again bring out deep emotions as we realise how dishonest we have been even with ourselves, but again it helps the process of integration with our higher consciousness. Once we have progressed on this process of integration we discover that we actually have no need to hide behind false façades because the real inner self is something that can feel solid, competent and complete with honesty and grace.

THIRD EYE EXERCISE

Place an object or set of objects on front of you. This could be a number of crystals, your athame, wand, or any other item. Use the normal process for entering a light meditation, then, with your physical eyes still closed, reach out with your receiving hand and pick up the object cleanly without fumbling around for it. With practice you should be able to do this every time. By 'tuning in' to the object using the third eye (and again I remind you that the secret is not to concentrate with the conscious mind) you will also be able to differentiate between the objects before you touch them.

To take this exercise a stage further you can work with an under-standing friend. It needs to be a close friend who has some understanding of your work, who is not someone you feel any need to impress, and who is not going to ridicule you in any way if at first you are less than successful. Your friend can move the object or objects around in front of you once you have your eyes shut. Take time to 'tune in' to the objects' energy then confidently pick that object up. You will find that you will also have to practice blocking out your friend's energy, a useful exercise in itself.

DANCING ON THE ASTRAL

We have already looked at the various planes of existence in the chapter on the Otherworld. This following exercise, whilst it is basically a bit of fun and an excellent way of relaxing and letting go, is also a good way to start learning how to actually enter the astral dimensions. This particular exercise should take you into the lower astral dimensions. The lower astral is generally the place of day dreams, though this is intended take you into that realm in a more controlled way.

You will need to find a piece of music to put on your stereo. I find it works best at a reasonably high volume, so maybe if you are likely to disturb anyone using a pair of headphones would be a good idea (although you don't want to be disturbed by someone creeping up on you). When you have used this technique by doing it in a relaxing atmosphere at home you may well find it possible to recreate it wherever you travel by using a Walkman (obviously not if you are driving). You can try it with any sort of music – the important thing is that it be a piece of music that you particularly like, and works best with a piece you are reasonably familiar with. Personally I like to use a lively piece of music – acid jazz is *my* favourite, but it *is* a personal choice.

Start off, as with other meditations, by sitting comfortably, calming one's mind and begin to enter the alpha state by clearing one's mind and using the breathing exercises as before. Turn on the music and allow yourself to be totally absorbed into the sounds; really get in to the music itself. Begin to visualise yourself against a plain backdrop where there are no physical restraints, including gravity. Start to visualise yourself dancing to the music in any way you like, remembering that you can completely let yourself go and do anything you want – in total privacy. Your limbs can move in any way, you can flip, fly, twist, turn, anything you want, just let the music inspire you to totally let go.

When you have finished, take some time to calm yourself down, return to normal breathing and ground yourself thoroughly.

ASTRAL TRAVELLING

Astral travelling takes the above exercise one stage further. Having practised visualisation you can begin to move out of your body and start to travel anywhere you like deeper on the astral plane. This can become quite involved, but it is necessary to build up to anything elaborate and at first keep it quite simple.

Begin a meditation in the normal way, making sure that you are sitting comfortably and totally relaxed. Start to visualise a double of yourself standing in front of yourself. Hold this visualisation for as long as you can and strengthen it as much as you can. When you feel ready, begin to transfer your consciousness into this double and look around from its perspective. Really look at yourself and look around the room seeing it as it was when you entered meditation. When you first start astral travelling it will be enough to hold this visualisation for as long as possible. The more you are able to hold the visualisation, the better you will become and what you are visualising will gradually become much more real and solid.

It is important to remember to return to your physical body at the end of any work of this kind.

When you become adept at holding the visualisation, you should find that you can move away from your physical body to any place you choose. On the astral you are not bound by time and space in the way we experience it on the physical plane. You can check your results by travelling on the astral to a place nearby that you have never been before – it could be a local shop, for instance. Enter the shop and have a good look around before coming back to your physical body. Later you can physically visit the shop and check to see if it is how you saw it on the astral (bearing in mind that any differences could be caused by moving through a different time).

Do not get carried away. Remember that the astral plane is a real plane, just a different one to the physical plane that we are more familiar with. All sorts of things can happen on the astral plane, just as they can on the physical, and you need to appreciate that this can affect you either positively or negatively just as it can on the physical.

Remember that you can return to your physical body at anytime, and should do so if you feel uneasy at any point. Remember also to ground yourself thoroughly after this sort of work.

BUILDING A PERSONAL ASTRAL TEMPLE

In the exercise above we used the astral to explore places on the physical dimension. However, as has been suggested before, the astral does not comply to the conventionally accepted concepts of time and space. It is therefore possible to create your own private space on the astral that you can use purely for yourself, or if you wish, take others through a guided meditation.

You can build yourself a personal temple on the astral plane that can be used as a sanctuary in which to work on oneself and to explore and develop deeper understanding of the elemental powers. Building such a temple is by definition 'personal', therefore what you build needs to be of your own design and everything within it should correspond with the symbology that you are both familiar and comfortable with. The following, therefore, is simply an example incorporating the common aspects that have been tried and tested by many on various paths. You will find that it is necessary to adapt it for your own needs. The astral temple is something that can be built over a long period, and changes can be made whenever you wish. It is certainly not necessary, or even advisable, to try and construct the whole elaborate visualisation in one go, but better to do it stage by stage allowing each session to build on that which was established before. Personally I find this is something that is best done before going to bed, though that is only a personal preference. The astral temple can be visited whenever you a have a desire or need.

Start each session by going into the standard meditational state before you move into visualisation mode. Remember to end each session by ensuring that you follow the same path out of the astral dimension that you took when you went into it.

Visualise yourself on a path in a wood. The path extends before you into the distance. Take time to see the trees in all their glory and experience the smell of the grass, trees and flowers. Hear the quiet business of the insects and other creatures working away unseen. Feel the breeze on your face gently blowing your hair.

When ready, begin to walk down the path until the trees suddenly stop and you find yourself on top of a cliff overlooking a wide clear plain. Nearby are steep steps that lead down. There are three flights of seven steps. Carefully walk down these steps, counting them as you go. When you reach the bottom, look ahead of you into the wide open plain and walk forward into it until you find a spot that feels good. Take some time to stand in this space. Look at the ground beneath your feet as well as looking out towards the horizon where gently rolling hills can be seen in the distance in all directions.

Establish which direction is East and sit down facing this direction to contemplate how you would like to use this peaceful place to build your own private temple to work in. It may eventually take any form. It could remain an open space, or maybe you will choose to construct a stone circle, or you may even prefer a tall strong tower.

Standing up again, walk to the East. See yourself walking through a place that represents the element associated with the East – the air. This may be a cloud, or a cliff top or a part of the plain where there is a strong

81

refreshing breeze. Keep a look out for an animal or item that represents the element of air to you and notice what happens and accept any gifts that are presented to you. You may, for instance, come across an eagle who settles down next to you and offers you a feather. Accept the feather and offer your thanks then take it back with you to your temple. Place the item in the East.

Repeat the previous excursion with the South, West and North (fire, water and earth). When you go to the South visualise yourself in a hot dry place, perhaps there is a volcano. In the West you may find yourself in a swamp or by a lake. In the North you may find a cave or a mine. You will eventually have four items representing the four elements placed around you with yourself, the fifth element of spirit, sat in the middle.

You can come back to this place at any time you want. When you come back you can use the temple to meditate, relax, build more. You can do anything you like and it can become as elaborate or as simple as your tastes demand. As mentioned before, when you have finished a work session in your temple, walk out the same way you came, especially remembering to walk up the steps. Walking down the steps when you enter helps to take you into a deeper level of meditation, strengthening the alpha state, therefore walking back up the steps, counting as you go, helps to bring yourself back to the waking beta state. Each time you return you will find that the temple is just as you left it before. As I have already said, it is *your* private and personal space that nobody can interfere with (unless you invite them to do so, which I recommend against, with the possible exception of a person who you totally trust and with whom you work extremely closely alongside).

11

THE COVEN

Many, in fact I would venture to suggest most, witches will find that the majority of their work is done alone as a solitary[21] even though strictly speaking Wicca itself is a group activity. The power and energy that can be raised when working with others, particularly those who you love and trust, can be quite amazing and should not be rejected, but considered carefully. Even if you do find it difficult finding others who you feel comfortable working with, being patient and exploring opportunities will be worth the effort.

A traditional witch coven consists of up to thirteen with a balance of male and female with the High Priestess generally making up the odd number. It can be seen as an extended family, the High Priestess playing the role of Mother. The High Priest usually acts as her assistant. All members will have a close bond to each other and as such it is necessary for the members to be chosen carefully so as not to threaten that bond in any way.

Those who have worked their way through the degree system and have been working witches for some years are looked upon as elders. It would be wrong to look upon the High Priestess, High Priest and any of the elders as 'superiors' as such, but more as one would look upon elders within a family situation – an equal member of the family, though most likely one who deserves their extended periods of dedication and effort to be valued and respected.

There are some covens, especially those amongst the Dianic path, that form themselves into all female groups and tend to concentrate on worshipping the Goddess aspects. Whilst I can appreciate the urge amongst women to do this, and there is a definite need after centuries of having been suppressed for all women to claim their full and rightful place in our communities, I don't personally feel that such a grouping can easily find the intrinsic balance integral to Wicca. Women throughout the

---

[21] A solitary witch is often referred to as a 'Hedgewitch'.

Age of Pisces have indeed suffered through a great deal of discrimination and misogyny. Even in the current era this has still not been overcome, though matters are slowly improving. It is useful, if not vital, for women to reassert themselves throughout all levels of modern society and for men to reassess their attitudes. However, witchcraft is essentially about balance, and I feel that such groupings, whilst capable of raising energy, are in danger of missing the point. The Old Religion was not a purely Goddess orientated path, despite what some feminists appear to believe. I can understand the temptation to redress the balance of past mistakes, but to reverse the roles of male and female in society is to produce a situation that for all intents and purposes is no better than what we had throughout the ages of male domination.

The Old Religion, at least whilst it was a partnership society, worshipped the Goddess and God in balance, with the Goddess playing a marginally leading role. The need for this balance should be obvious to all on an esoteric path. Properly balanced groups do not disregard the possibility, or the need, for the female members (or male members for that matter) to work on their own at times to discuss their own specific issues and mysteries and work for their own goals – but I feel strongly that the full coven should contain a reasonable balance of both male and female energy. Working magic is, after all, about working with a firm balance between the two polarities.

One of the roles of the High Priestess and the High Priest, who would normally be the first members of any coven, is to gradually draw to themselves those who may in future become part of the coven. Evangelism is something that is most definitely frowned upon in Wicca, though being open and available for those who seek such a path is important. In any coven situation there will usually be a number of cowans (someone who is not initiated) in some form of outer circle to the coven. There is nothing wrong with inviting cowans to observe from outside of a Circle working, or even attend within the Circle, though I would restrict this to Esbats and Sabbats and not full ritual magical workings where the energy flows can be particularly volatile and best handled by the more experienced. Whilst there are few rules to witchcraft, there are many responsibilities that are essential to adhere to if success is to be achieved in one's work and unintentional psychological damage to outsiders is to be avoided.

In the coven there are often two other roles that are often fulfilled by member Priestesses. These are the roles of Maiden and Crone. The Maiden would normally be a youthful and physically attractive member who acts as hand-maiden to the High Priestess and High Priest undertaking some of the roles such as preparing the candles, etc. The Crone would normally be an older elder of the coven, possibly a former High Priestess herself.

Together with the High Priestess the three embody the traditional Triple Goddess aspects of Maiden, Mother and Crone.

Despite the 'posts' within the circle, witchcraft is not generally a hierarchical religion. Covens are individual units answerable only to themselves under the guidance of High Priestess and High Priest and as such through them to the gods. The fact that covens are individual units, responsible only to themselves, is one of the strengths of witchcraft whilst at the same time a potential weakness, especially if the High Priestess and/or High Priest are not adequately advanced. Certainly in times of persecution having individual covens with little contact would have rendered it nearly impossible to entirely wipe out those following the Craft and limit the damage when the inquisition uncovered a coven. Today it also means that even if one coven folds, as inevitably many will, it does not have a ripple effect amongst those around it. If Wicca became hierarchical, with national figureheads dictating to the 'lower rankings' then it would become no better than the Christian Church and would destroy the very necessary individuality and variety that is fundamental to each individual's spiritual development. It is essential to the very essence of witchcraft that it remains diverse and (to a certain extent) anarchical. Paganism is a deeply personal religion. For the purposes of development it is essential that each individual is allowed to develop their own image of the way the cosmos works and is shaped as our minds all work in different ways and with different images. It is vital that access to 'the divine' is not distanced by a hierarchical system but that every single person clearly understands that they have equal access through their own minds. This does not mean that we have different ideals or theories about what constitutes the 'truth', though many will argue that we do until we are blue in the face more often than not, but it does mean that many of us will have different names for certain energies, and anthropomorphise to a greater or lesser extent. There are no 'right' ways or 'wrong' ways, only different.

The High Priestesses and High Priests within the Craft are those who have progressed through to the third degree. Within a Circle situation they often play the roles of Goddess and God in ceremonies and have those energies invoked into them during ritual. They must recognise that they have no authority over others, but as elders do have a great many responsibilities. One of the greatest responsibilities is to ensure that they are there not so much to teach but to help guide those who ask for assistance in the direction where they may find the answers; and as third degree elders they should have overcome egotistical problems enough to not deter someone they are guiding from reaching their own level or even superseding it. They should be on hand to help when help is asked for, and respect privacy when it is not.

Those joining the coven will be those who have been introduced through the right guidance to get them there. They should associate themselves (not by force or suggestion, but by personal choice) to a reasonable set of deity images be they Celtic, Nordic, Egyptian, Italian or whatever.

Mixing deity sets is another matter that I consider to be a mistake. Chanting to "Isis, Astarte, Diana, Hecate, Demeter, Kali and Innana" is all very well for the new age pagan who feels the need to invoke feminine energies, but in doing so one is calling on Goddess images from a wide range of cultures and belief systems. It is important if one is to thoroughly raise energy in the strongest possible way to tune into the collective group soul of our ancestors and not cloud the issue by over enthusiastic ecelecticism. I am not saying that mixing traditions will not raise energy for the work at hand, but that energy will be less focused and diminished than work in tune with one that has a proper understanding of the tradition one follows. Rules can be broken, but to the detriment of the participants and the well-intended work they undertake. It is ultimately the High Priestess and the High Priest who should take on the responsibility of ensuring these matters are carefully considered and offer advice when necessary. This is just one reason why those officers need to have worked and studied hard to achieve their positions of responsibility and must have reached an age where they have become mature enough to take such responsibilities objectively. I doubt that it is possible (though I may be mistaken) for somebody to have reached a level a maturity suitable for becoming a High Priestess or High Priest below the age of thirty. This would fit in well with the ideas expressed within the circles of esoteric psychology. At the age of eighteen or twenty-one, having survived adolescence, the education system, our parent bonds, and found ourselves earning our own money and 'independent' it is easy for us to believe that we have reached maturity. Few at such an age will be able to convince us otherwise. That doesn't change the fact that we actually have many lessons and a great deal of maturing ahead of us. We may well have evolved into mature individuals on the physical plane, but at that sort of age we are only beginning to develop beyond the ego and the Self on the elemental plane.

Another responsibility of the High Priestess and High Priest within a Coven is to carefully monitor and make decisions as to when members are ready to be initiated into the Circle and when those already within it are ready (if ever) to move up to the second degree or beyond (see chapter on rites of passage for more discussion and details of the initiation process). There is no set time for this process, although traditionally a year and a day is the minimum that it is likely to take though some will be quicker, many much slower, and others still many never progress further at all.

The High Priestess and High Priest, having reached the third degree of initiation, the last in the initiation process, they will be aware that it is far from the last step they will take on the road to development. It is a stage where one realises actually how little one really understands and that there are in fact seven levels of development rather than three – the seventh only ever reachable having left the current physical incarnation and moved to the Other World. They will bear in mind the truth behind the words 'He who thinks he knows everything, knows nothing . . .'

The following was taken from Raymond Buckland's *Complete Book of Witchcraft*, itself from an unknown source. I have used it here because it sums up the demanding attitude that every High Priestess and High Priest should strive to achieve:

You may come to them for a few moments,
Then go away and do whatever you will;
Their love is unchanging.

You may deny them to themselves or to yourself,
Then curse them to any who will listen;
Their love is unchanging.

You may become the enemy of the gods themselves,
Then return to them;
Their love is unchanging.

Go where you will;
Stay however long you will and come back to them;
Their love is unchanging.

Abuse others; abuse yourself;
Abuse them and come back to them;
Their love is unchanging.

They will never criticise you;
They will never minimise you;
They will never fail you,
Because to them you are everything and they themselves are nothing.
They will never deceive you;
They will never ridicule you;
They will never fail you,
Because to them you are God/Goddess-nature,
To be served and they are your servants.

No matter what befalls you,
No matter what you become,
They await you always.

They know you; they serve you; they love you.
Their love for you, in the changing world is unchanging.
Their love, beloved, is unchanging.

When acting as High Priestess and High Priest one is representing the Goddess and God. The God, as the Sun, brings the force that the Mother Goddess, as the Earth, utilises to bring forth life in the spring, blossoming into full fruit in the summer, and then nurturing the seed safe in her womb (underground) throughout the winter when the Sun's energy is withdrawn and less powerful. It is working on this principle that the God (represented in the circle through the High Priest) provides the energy for the Goddess (represented through the High Priestess) to perform the work. The High Priestess draws on the High Priest for energy as each of us is a perfect microcosm of nature. The High Priest gives his energy to be used wisely in perfect love and perfect trust readily enabling balance between the polarities. If, however, the High Priest for some reason loses faith and trust in his High Priestess to use their combined energy for the good of all and chooses to withdraw it then the matter needs to be discussed fully and (hopefully) the situation resolved in a mature fashion, otherwise the coven needs to either rearrange itself or the participants move on to pastures new.

FINDING A TEACHER

If you have already made contact with a High Priestess or High Priest, and you have chosen wisely, then you will already have found the ideal person to guide you through your development. I say 'guide' because that is a much better word than 'teach'. A good teacher will rarely sit you down and give you exercises. He or she will more often encourage you to find your own way, answer your questions when you ask them, and let you get on with it when you don't.

No matter how much you respect the person who is teaching you, never accept what they have to say blindly. Always question everything and be prepared to disagree if something doesn't feel right. Never put them on a pedestal – even the most adept magus is fallible and it is not necessarily the case that the symbolism that you feel comfortable with is in tune with that of your teacher. There are many ways to tread the path of enlightenment, all equally as valid as the next. You have to be sure that your teacher is guiding you down a path that you feel in tune with, otherwise don't be afraid to find a new teacher and/or a new path, however difficult that may seem.

12

TOOLS OF THE CRAFT

There are a number of 'tools' traditionally used in witchcraft. As you become more adept at your Craft you will discover that these tools aren't entirely necessary. The power of the witch comes from the witch and the energies that are tapped into by her/him. The tools are simply used as an aid to focus and for ceremonial as well as ritual purposes.

The best tools are ones that you have made yourself. Putting your own energy into the item and personalising it makes it special to you and reflects your own character. Remember these descriptions are only for guidance. There are no rules. If you prefer, as Terry Pratchett's Granny Weatherwax does, to use an everyday bread knife as an athame instead, then that is up to you! Have fun making and choosing your tools. Keep them special and sacred to you. Do not let anyone outside of your own circle touch them or use them. It is best that your own energy remains in them and does not become tainted with others. When not in use, keep them in a special place. Somewhere near your altar is probably best. If you have drawers under your altar, then this can become an extension of the altar itself and is a good place to store your Book of Shadows, tools, divination instruments such as crystal balls, tarot cards, dark mirrors, candles, incense and anything else you use for your worship and work.

CONSECRATION OF TOOLS

Tools used by a witch are consecrated before the Gods before they are used. This needn't be done within a full Circle, though it is best if it is. To do so, stand before the altar and use words along the lines of . . .

> *'Lord and Lady, Goddess and God,*
> *I [Chosen name]*[22] *am your Witch and Priest[ess],*

---

[22] For an explanation of chosen names see 'Magical Numbers and Magic Name' in this chapter and the section on Initiation in chapter 18 on 'Rites of Passage'.

I am of you, as you are of me.
I consecrate this tool in your names,
To aid me in my work.
For the good of all,
according to the free will of all,
So it must be.'

The tool in question is then passed three times through the flame of a candle, three times through the smoke of incense, and sprinkled with already salted water, thus consecrating it with the elements of fire, air, earth and water.

AMULETS AND TALISMANS

Amulets and Talismans take many forms and include crystals, runes, jewellery and are usually constructed from organic material rather than synthetics such as plastic. Amulets are designed to protect the wearer from unwanted influences. Talismans draw energy to the wearer. Both work on the spiritual, elemental and psychological level.

ATHAME

The athame is one of the main tools used in Wiccan magic. The athame is a ritual knife used to direct one's will as is the wand. It is used to cast the Circle and often used to summon the Guardians of the Elements within a Circle setting. It is used in the right hand (if right-handed) which is your sending or power hand when directing your energies, and the left when receiving as when you 'pick up' a cast Circle at the end of a ritual or ceremony.

Raymond Buckland, in *Buckland's Complete Book of Witchcraft*, ventures to suggest that the athame can be used to replace the need for a wand at all. However, the problem with this is that certain elements and spirits do not respond to iron and in such cases an athame would not be suitable. One would certainly not be wanting to be so presumptuous as to 'demand' the presence of the Goddess and God, bearing in mind it is used to direct one's will, by using one's athame which would be disrepectful.

Traditionally it is a black-handled knife with a double sided blade. It needn't necessarily be sharp, but as it represents air (and thus the intellect) personally I prefer mine to be sharp. One's intellect and will should surely be best represented by a tool that is sharp! As with all tools of the Craft, it is better that you make your own and thus put your own energy and personality into the athame.

Being made of iron or steel, the athame builds up energy put into it by your usage of it. For this reason nobody else, other than one's High

Priestess or High Priest should touch or use your own personal athame. Sticking the athame into ground will discharge the energies built up in the tool by grounding it. Laying one's athame against an athame belonging to another witch will charge the athame with some of that witch's energy. The athame can also be charged by using it at ancient centres of power such as stone circles.

BOLEEN

A Boleen is traditionally a white-handled knife, more often than not with a curved blade. It is not often used within a Circle, but more commonly used as a working tool for cutting herbs at the appropriate time. It should be a knife that you use only for herbs and other items gathered from nature so that one shows respect by using a consecrated tool. Personally I use a modern sharp pocket knife with a silver handle which is much easier to carry around.

BOOK OF SHADOWS

A Book of Shadows is a book used by each individual witch to contain notes regarding the work they do within the Craft. Traditionally it contains copies of the rituals, ceremonies and spells used by that witch. If the witch is part of a Coven then it can also be used to copy from the Coven's own joint Book of Shadows after initiation so that the knowledge built up by Coven is shared and passed on.

Traditionally the Book of Shadows is prepared in the witch's own hand-writing. In the days of persecution this would have been so that if a witch were accused by the inquisition and the book found, then no other Coven member could be held responsible. A book would obviously have been burnt in such a situation if an opportunity arose in order to protect the occult knowledge contained within it.

In these enlightened and modern times, I see absolutely no reason why a Book of Shadows cannot be prepared on a word processor if that is one's normal mode of writing as it is for many these days. If you choose this method – always keep a back-up copy!

BROOM

A traditional witch's broom is known as a besom. The handle represents the phallus, thus the male element joined with the female element of the brush. It is a representation of the essential balance between masculine and feminine, and can be used to represent the element of air.

It is sometimes used within a ritual situation to help visualise the cleansing of an area to be used for a Circle casting before the altar is prepared. It can also be used during certain ceremonies such as a hand-fasting where it is used to represent the domestic joining of male and female.

You will often find a besom standing at the front door of the house of a witch. Traditionally it is the first item brought into a new home, and the last to leave. This represents the cleansing of the new home and is often a sign to others of the presence of a witch.

CAULDRON

The cauldron, represents the womb of the Goddess in the same way as the Chalice. It is not an essential item, but can be used during certain rituals and spell-work. The cauldron appears symbolically in many of the Celtic myths.

CHALICE

The Chalice is used within many rituals, and often forms an element on the altar. It represents the womb of the Goddess and as such it can be used as part of a representation of such during spell-work and rituals. As it generally contains water or wine it can also be used to represent the element of water.

CORDS

Cords are part of a Wiccan's ceremonial costume and usually also a mark of the initiation level of that witch although sometimes the colour is a matter for personal taste. They are traditionally nine feet long (being a sacred number three times three) and vary in colour. Different traditions use different colour schemes. I suggest the use of white for the first initiation (representing purity), red or green for the second initiation (red representing life, green the connection with the Earth or Mars as masculine and Venus as feminine) and silver or gold for the third (representing the office of the High Priestess or High Priest).

The cords also represent the circle, and thus the connection with all things. They are tied with a reef knot (left over right, right over left) symbolising the connection with the left and right elements of the brain, and the interdependence of the masculine and feminine principles. The ends of the cords dangle centrally in front of the wearer representing the umbilical cord and the connection with the Mother Goddess. The reef knot is a symbolic representation of the hexagram – or six-pointed star – and contains all of that symbol's associations.

Cords can also be used for various magical practices that involve tying knots (binding one's wishes and intent) and within Coven work they can be used as a tool to help raise energy by passing them around and dancing with them in various ways.

As part of your sacred costume used on special occasions when you show respect for the gods and nature, keep the cords in a special place where they will not become damaged, preferably in a drawer under or near your altar, or with your robes.

CRYSTALS

Crystals hold and emanate Earth energies of many different types that can be readily tapped into by a witch. Their correspondences need to be carefully considered before using them in your work, to which they add a great deal of energy indeed. Crystals can be charged up in your power hand (right hand if right-handed) and the energies can be drawn upon when needed in your other hand. They can also be charged up by leaving them outside under a Full Moon. They can be cleansed, as they need to be on a regular basis, by holding them under running water.

DIVINATION AND DIVINATION TOOLS

There are a great many tools in the witch's armoury that can be used for divination. They include tarot cards, crystal balls, black mirrors, runes, staves and stones (of which there are many types). Unfortunately I cannot, in this book, even begin to go into the subject of divination which is so vast a subject that it requires at least one volume of its own. What I will say, however, is that divination is a skill that most witches develop and use thoroughly. One should remember that when using divination tools, what is seen should never be seen as fate but as the outcome of whatever the current set of circumstances permit – which can obviously be changed.

HERBS AND HERBALISM

The use of herbs and herbalism is common amongst witches. Becoming familiar with the uses of herbs for healing and ritual use is both a useful occupation for a witch and yet another way of getting in tune with the natural energies prevalent in the hedgerow. Again, the subject is far too large to be entered into through a book like this, but any witch worth their salt would include a few good herbals in their book collection, and may even take the subject so far as to start a herbal notebook of their own.

Herbs contain elements that can have a significant effect on the healing process when required. The natural energies stored in herbs are powerful and drawn directly from the Earth and the rest of the surrounding environment as well as from the air and the sun. Many witches build up a knowledge of herbs, their uses and correspondences and have an extensive collection that can be utilised in healing, and made into incenses for special occasions. (See appendices.)

MAGIC NUMBERS AND MAGIC NAMES

One of the first things we tend to do in Wicca is to choose a new name for ourselves.

Magic numbers are used to represent names with the numerical value of each letter worked out using the chart below that is based on a grid of nine (a sacred number being three times three, three being the number representing the Goddess in her triple aspect). In numerology one reduces numbers to a single figure by adding them together, and adding the resulting number together again, until the number is reduced to just a single figure. My given name – KEVIN – would initially be represented by the numbers 25495. From this one gets $2 + 5 + 4 + 9 + 5 = 25$, then $2 + 5 = 7$.

1	2	3	4	5	6	7	8	9
A	B	C	D	E	F	G	H	I
J	K	L	M	N	O	P	Q	R
S	T	U	V	W	X	Y	Z	

Your birth number is worked out from the date on which you were born. Mine is 23rd October 1960. From this you would derive your birth number in the same way as above – 23101960. This becomes – $2 + 3 + 1 + 0 + 1 + 9 + 6 + 0 = 24$ and then $2 + 4 = 6$. This then is my magical birth number and relates to a system of numerology, a vast subject of its own.

When we become initiated as a witch, it is usual to pick a new name for oneself. The given name is one that our parents chose for us. Choosing a name for ourselves allows us to create around that name a personality – a magical personality – or our own. This is used in witch-craft as the name one is known by within Circle work. The name is not normally given out to anyone outside of your own Circle as it is under-stood that those who know your true name have power over you if they are unscrupulous enough to choose to use it. To derive one's Chosen Name we first refer back to the birth number. Mine being 6, I would then take any combination of letters that would allow me to end up with a reduced number of 6 and use these letters to make up a chosen name from them.

PENTACLE

The pentacle is a round, flat, copper, brass or wooden disc, usually larger than six-inches in diameter, upon which a pentagram[23] is inscribed, painted or carved on it. It usually sits in a central position on the altar representing the element of earth. The pentacle is used to contain a charged energy which is passed on to any small item that is placed upon it. The pentacle receives energy through work concentrated through it during meditation in front of the altar, direct energy input working directly with the pentacle, through being a focal point during rituals, and if used in a Coven situation, from energy put into it by other Coven members.

As well as a pentagram, the Pentacle is often also decorated with other sigils and runes to personalise it. These can include a bind rune[24] of the owner of the Pentacle, symbols for the elements of Earth, Air, Fire and Water, and any other symbols that are used regularly by the users of the altar.

ROBES

Robes are the sacred costume used on ceremonial or ritual occasions. They can be any colour or design as they are an expression of the individual. As part of the process of getting one's mind in the appropriate frame for ritual work, one may find that several sets of robes are built up, different colours chosen to be appropriate for the occasion.

They should ideally be made by the witch who intends to wear them, again putting one's own energy into them. They should always be treated with respect and kept in a safe place. Ideally, when required, they should be hand washed so that one's own energy is reinforced into the fabric. It is best to use natural materials such as cotton as this helps to conduct natural energies. One would not normally wear anything under the ritual costume so that interference with natural energy flows is kept to a minimum.

SCOURGE

The scourge or flail is a tool used in some traditions of the Craft, though it is not one I have ever used, or likely to use. It is basically a small whip made of nine lengths or cord or leather, each nine inches long and each tied with nine knots. In Covens that use the scourge it is used for purification purposes. It would seem to have been first introduced by Gerald

---

[23] For further information on the pentagram refer to the chapter 'The Elements'.

[24] A 'bind rune' is one that has been made up from combining several runes together.

Gardner's original texts, and continued into Alexandrain rituals. Gardner seemed particularly keen on the use of this instrument. However, I see no need for it in the modern context and feel that its associations are not suitable for modern Wicca.

WAND

The wand, like the athame, is used by a witch to direct energies. Whereas the athame is associated with the element of air, the wand is associated with the element of fire. Its symbolism is phallic and therefore masculine and associated with God elements.

A wand can be made from a small branch from any sort of wood. The tree correspondences should be taken into account when choosing one. Some within the Craft say that the length of a wand should be the same as that from the tip of one's little finger to the elbow. Personally I don't find that this is particularly important. The wood used should ideally come off easily in one's hand from the tree in question – the tree shown respect and thanked when this happens. The wand can then be stripped of its bark (if you feel that is right) and decorated with runes, personalised bind runes, or other protective sigils.

13

THE RULES OF WITCHCRAFT

The only 'rule' in Wicca is *'If it harm none, do what you will.'* For the sake of completeness the following is a version of the Wiccan Rede as it generally appears in a traditional Gardnerian Book of Shadows

> *Bide ye Wiccan laws ye must*
> *in perfect love and perfect trust*
> *Live and let live, fairly take, fairly give*
> *Form the circle thrice about to keep all evil spirits out*
> *To bind ye spell every time, let ye spell be spoke in rhyme*
> *Soft of eye, light of touch, speak ye little, listen much*
> *Deosil go by the waxing moon, singing out ye Witches' Rune*
> *Widdershins go by the waning moon, chanting out ye Baneful Rune*
> *When the moon rides at her peak, then ye heart's desire seek*
> *Heed the North wind's mighty gale, lock the door and trim the sail*
> *When the wind comes from the South, love will kiss thee on the mouth*
> *When the wind blows from the West, departed souls may have no rest*
> *When the wind blows from the East, expect the new and set the feast*
> *Nine woods in ye cauldron go, burn them fast and burn them slow*
> *Elder be ye Lady's tree, burn it not or cursed ye'll be*
> *When the wheel begins to turn, soon ye Beltane fire'll burn*
> *When the wheel hath turned to Yule, light a log the Horned One rules*
> *Heed ye flower, bush and tree, by the Lady blessed be*
> *Where the rippling waters flow, cast a stone and truth ye'll know*
> *When ye have and hold a need, harken not to other's greed*
> *With a fool no season spend, nor be counted as his friend*
> *Merry meet and merry part, bright the cheeks and warm the heart*
> *When misfortune is anow, wear the blue star upon thy brow*
> *True in love ye must ever be, lest the love be false to thee*
> *In these eight words the Wiccan Rede fulfill;*
> *If it harm none, do what ye will.*

Contrary to popular belief, or at least what many seem to believe, 'do what you will' is not meant to be a licence for anarchy. The will is intended to mean – whatever it is you are meant to do in this life – or more accurately, the Will of the Higher Self determined by the divine. This could be a number of things – bringing up and teaching children; teaching others; helping the sick or elderly; helping to protect the environment; all sorts of things. Basically what it is saying is – use whatever means you need to do what you need to do, as long as it doesn't harm others.

Gerald Gardner almost certainly got his inspiration, as he did whilst filling in many of the gaps found in the traditional witchcraft teachings that he received, from Aleister Crowley. Crowley published a set of magical principles in his 'Book of Thelema' which (it is claimed) was channelled to him through his spiritual guide. This material concludes with the words 'Do what thou wilt shall be the whole of the law.' That is – do what one is willed. Whatever the true source of the Rede, if one accepts that the Higher Self, as an element of the divine, chose this incarnation as part of the work set by the divine Will, then undertaking the will as determined by one's Higher Self is a perfectly reasonable undertaking. This is yet another reason why personal self-development must be a foundation stone in Wicca and any other esoteric path, for unless we are able, through consistent work and effort, to fully awaken the senses to the Higher Self and one's guides then it is impossible to fully determine what the true 'will' is.

Unfortunately none of us are perfect. Doing our best and striving for perfection is the best we can do, it is all that the gods expect of us, and when we do mess up we need to learn from our mistakes so that we may strive not to repeat them.

As part of your meditation regime, think about things you have done that have had a negative effect on those around you, or that have harmed nature in some way. Accept that there are things you have done that have caused harm (everyone has to some degree or another) and consider these matters in detail. Think what you could have done, or should have done, that could have effected a better and less damaging outcome. However, having recognised this, rather than wallowing in blame and guilt, know that having considered this that you have learnt an important lesson that will help you handle matters better in future – and if there are things that can be done to repair any damage you have caused – do it.

There are many who will tell us that you must do things in certain ways. In many of the Wiccan traditions the words used in circles, and the names of the Goddesses and Gods are pre-ordained. This, however, is a big mistake.

One of the main aims of being a witch is to attain harmony and balance within yourself and, by doing so, helping to bring harmony and balance to all that are around you and that you come in contact with. Much of the personal work is, therefore, psychological. Throughout meditations, ritual work, spell casting, etc, we are working to thoroughly connect the conscious mind with the sub-conscious and through that one's Higher Self. The sub-conscious mind does not recognise words, but symbols. Therefore, unless you find the symbols that mean something to you – to your sub-conscious – (and we are all different) your work will not have the desired effect. The best way to find the appropriate symbols is to follow your intuition. Your intuition is after all controlled by your sub-conscious.

There are of course tried and tested methods for casting circles, casting spells, elementals to invoke, tools to use – those that have worked for me I have shared with you through this book. I do not expect you to copy everything that I do, nor is it required that you do things my way or anyone else's for that matter.

Study the wisdom of others and then do what feels right to you – 'do what you will'.

WHAT IS A WITCH?

There are a great many definitions as to what constitutes a witch. There are many traditions to choose from – there are many paths to the same goal, none are necessarily better or worse than others. There is not a right way or a wrong way, but many individual and different ways.

But what is the difference between a pagan and a witch in its modern sense?

As far I am concerned, a pagan is somebody who worships, or at least venerates, nature and worships the two polarities of Goddess and God through nature and is at least aware of the natural energy flows. Paganism includes all the various traditions of druidry, shamanism and witchcraft, as well as those who are simply just pagan. Being a pagan (or neopagan) means that one endeavours to live one's life showing respect for the Goddess (or aspects of the Goddess and various goddesses) and God as they were determined in pre-Christian times. Neopaganism is defined by the *Oxford English Dictionary* as 'a modern religious movement which seeks to incorporate beliefs or ritual practices from traditions outside the main world religions, especially those of pre-Christian Europe and North America.' A witch is a pagan who goes one step further and uses the energies provide by the goddesses and gods to further their work and a Wiccan is a modern form of witchcraft that follows a system of development, generally within a group situation (or at least with guidance from elders) in a form derived initially from the teachings passed on by Gerald Gardner in the 1950s.

Being a witch means that one uses nature's energies from all the planes of existence to perform 'magic'. It is a calling that is not going to be heeded by all pagans — it takes a lot of dedication and commitment. When one becomes a Wiccan Priestess or Priest you are putting yourself in a position of responsibility, to work with the gods within and throughout all, for the good of all — at least within your own 'community'[25]. A witch is a wise person of the Craft — and uses the abilities that she or he develops through her or his training not for personal gain, but for the good of all. It is an unselfish undertaking to aid the work of the gods as their servant. As part of this work a witch ensures that her or his *real* needs (as opposed to unnecessary material gratifications) are catered for because inevitably such needs enable one to undertake this work.

As far as I am concerned, being a witch is an ability to use the natural energies with a grounding in the faith of nature, and with proper guidance from the gods, contact with which is made through your spiritual higher consciousness. A witch is a magician, though a magician is not necessarily a witch, there are other faiths that enable contact with the spiritual higher consciousness[26]. However, a so-called magician who is not guided by the spirit within who uses natural energies is not a magician at all, but merely a 'sorcerer' who risks building a great deal of negative karma that will rebound and have to be dealt with at some point either in this incarnation or another.

THE THREE-FOLD LAW OF RETURN

A law that is recognised by the witch and ignored at their own peril, is the Three-fold Law. It states that whatever one gives out returns to the sender three times over. This is a natural law rather than a philosophical guiding principle and as such applies whether one believes in it or not.

It is also a law that appears to be much misunderstood, just as with the Wiccan Rede. On the face of it one may consider it to be a threat that if one were to undertake bad deeds then one will be a victim of that negativity as a punishment. Whilst it is true that the negativity will hit the perpetrator with three times the force of that which is originally

---

[25] By 'community' I mean the personal community with which you associate, not necessarily just the locality within which you physically live.
[26] Modern Wicca itself draws on techniques drawn from other magical paths that are not in themselves pagan.

put into the deed, it is not true that it is a punishment from some outside force. Once again, the truth lies within the individual. Any intentional negativity generated by a person will tend to stick in the mind of that person and affect them on a mental level. From the mental level it will filter through to affect them on a spiritual level and also on the physical level. It is purely a psychological process rather than a deeply mystical one. It is understanding this law that ensures that the wise witch works for the common good rather than manipulating the powers of nature for personal gain at the expense of others, or to seek retribution for malice aimed at them.

The wise witch recognising this law will simply protect themselves from any malice by ensuring that the negativity aimed at them is reflected directly back at the sender who themselves will suffer from the Three-fold Law with no effect on the intended target.

This law, of course, does more than merely protect oneself from negativity through such reflection, or teach the perpetrators of any such malice through the suffering of their own negativity. The law also works with positive energy. If a person dedicates their life to doing good deeds for those around them, or for the common good as a whole, that positive energy will also manifest through themselves on the mental, spiritual and physical level. So not only is it a law that discourages bad needs, it encourages good.

An aspect of witchcraft that is attractive to the immature within our materialistic culture, and one that is encouraged by a host of commercially orientated esoteric writers, is the idea of being able to use the powers of nature to gain money or manipulate the love of a potential partner. One of the first things that a Wiccan undertakes on their path before they even reach the position of being initiated to the first degree, is to dedicate themselves to the Goddess and God. Without such a dedication, the potential initiate will fail to learn what witchcraft is all about and will thus be unable to fully tune themselves to the energies that they will later use to work magic.

Techniques of visualisation, backed up by the intent focused through the use of certain words (or 'spells' as they are generally presented) can have a certain degree of success, at least initially. If one calls on the Gods for a wealth of money and enough energy is put into the visualisation and the intent, it may well be rewarded by some success. But it is highly unlikely that any money forthcoming will bring any great satisfaction. It is more likely to bring misery in the long run either by expecting to be continually rewarded with similar amounts of cash, and when it is no longer forthcoming suffering years of debts; or by the realisation that despite the promises made by the false gods worshipped in this modern world of materialism and unfettered commerce that money doesn't buy happiness.

Love may also be attracted by such methods with some degree of success. Equally hard lessons are likely to be learnt through such manipulation as the love attracted is unlikely to be based on anything deep and solid, but more often on something as fickle as lust. Such relationships, if they work at all, are doomed to failure bringing the misery that is deserved through abusing the powers of nature. Love can be attracted to the individual only when it is not directed at a particular individual, but based on attraction of being a sincerely nice, honest person who is confident and able to love themselves. If one cannot love oneself, how can anyone truly expect anyone else to love them?

Witches are taught that manipulation of others is something to be avoided at all costs. It is something that will almost certainly be subject to the Three-fold Law with the resulting self-punishment as the final product. There is no protection from this law, as it is a law of nature. To teach a young witch that they should never undertake any such manipulation is a vital guiding principle. They may well express despair and claim that if one can't use the magical powers of nature that there is no point in being a witch. This is, however, merely an expression of their own immaturity and a sign that they are not ready to learn the ways of the occult – the hidden inner powers of the human mind. It is only natural that a young person reaching towards maturity and just discovering how their society and the world works should think like this. It is all part of growing up, but it is also the reason why any serious coven of witches should resist introducing anyone under the age of 18, and even at that age should they be careful to ensure that the individual is of an exceptionally mature mind with righteous intentions.

THE EIGHT-FOLD WAY

The Eight-Fold Way is recognised in other esoteric paths with certain variations and is discussed more fully throughout this book. The Eight-Fold Way' constitutes the many ways of raising energy that are incorporated into the ritual magic performed by a witch, and represent the eight-spoked wheel upon which Wicca turns.

1. MENTAL DISCIPLINE

Powerful energies can be raised through the mind using meditation and trance. Visualisation can help apply the pure will of the mind over matter. By developing our mental ability we tap into energies that have always been available to us, through ones that we have not necessarily been aware of. Visualisation is one of the most important aspects of magical work. Stimulating all five of the senses one can utilise the art of visualisation to raise energy and transform it to all manner of ends. Visualisation comes easier to some than others, but it is an art that all should endeavour to develop and practise regularly. Mental discipline is also gained through cleansing the body (including fasting over short periods) and physical discipline). Ritual knowledge is also a vital aspect of mental discipline. Knowledge helps provide the keys that we need to help get in touch with our higher selves and beyond, as well as the knowledge and understanding we require in order to use enchantments, spells, symbols and charms.

2. THE POWER OF SPEECH

Speech is used in ritual to help strengthen the visualisation and thus the power of one's will. Chants can help to focus the mind and raise energy in their own way by penetrating the veil between the worlds. When using speech during a ritual, speak clearly, with feeling and confidence.

3. THE CONTROLLED USE OF DRUGS

The controlled use of drugs is something that seems to have played a part in most of the nature-based religions from all over the planet. Shamans from many cultures used hallucinogens to focus the mind and to aid the process of shape-shifting. Cannabis has also been used for centuries in magical work, as have several other natural substances readily available in the British Isles such as particular types of mushroom. Wine, beer, incense, essential oils and herbs also come into the realm of drugs (incenses also stimulate the olfactory glands in the nose). Whilst personally I find the laws against the use of cannabis quite ludicrous, especially for medical use (when drugs such as morphine and valium are legal and commonplace) I cannot advocate its use or that of any other illegal drug for fear of committing incitement. Some drugs are very potent, and if you do choose to experiment with them please do so with the utmost of caution.

4. DANCE

Dance is another way of raising energy, particularly useful in a circle situation. There are many dances that have become associated with the particular rites within Wicca. Dances often start slowly and build up tempo to a crescendo. This is associated with raising the cone of power especially in full Circle work.

5. OFFERINGS TO THE GODS

In the past many blood offerings were presented for the gods. This is not something that is generally advocated in modern witchcraft. Today it is more common to offer bread, wine, incense and crystals. Through offerings we are giving back something of value to the gods to thank them for what they have provided for us. Offerings more often consist of things that have personal value and are given as a form of sacrifice to show respect and to strengthen our connection with the goddesses and gods and nature spirits.

6. THE SCOURGE/PURIFICATION

The scourge is used in some forms of Wicca to beat energy into an object or to purify an individual through mildly inflicted pain. Flagellation is a common form of ritual purification found in many cultures and religions. It is not something I personally use or advocate because of its modern associations with sexual perversities. However, purification of the body IS important. One should cleanse one's body regularly. Salt is commonly used by witches for this purpose as is incense for purifying the aura. One should never enter a situation where one is working with the gods and spirits without having cleansed and purified oneself – it is a matter of respect for yourself and respect towards them.

7. SEX

The sexual act of a man and a woman is regarded as the sacred merging of the two great powers of masculine and feminine. It can be a most powerful way of raising energy within a ritual situation when performed with reverence and focus. Sex is not something I generally advocate in magic except between a man and a woman who are normally sexual partners and are both reasonably adept.

8. PSYCHIC DEVELOPMENT

Psychic development, dream control and other astral work is something that should develop through the training of a Wiccan if such abilities are not already developed before one begins. When working ritual magic, one is working between the worlds with the gods and spirits of the elemental planes, etc. It is therefore necessary to develop such skills if one is to become adept at working with such entities.

14

GODDESSES AND GODS

There are many 'pagan' belief systems that are in general use today. It is not the case that one is right and the others wrong, they are just different. Having said they are different, to be accurate they tend to have a basic starting point in that pagans are both monotheistic (they believe in one divine source) and polytheistic (they see this one source manifest as various elements or god forms, usually divided between masculine and feminine energies as goddesses and gods).

There are, however, many belief systems that fall into the category of 'paganism' (I use the word in its generally accepted modern context as a spiritual belief system based on nature worship). There are those who simply worship an individualised concept of the Goddess and God – often taking onboard a whole mixture of deity figures from a whole host of former belief systems which I find very confusing and not entirely helpful in developing an association. Others may have looked to what they have learnt from history within the culture they feel most strongly associated with and taken onboard a system that is based on Egyptian, Roman, Greek, Norse or Celtic goddesses and gods. Personally I use the Celtic deities that have their roots in the culture of Britain and Ireland, as that is where I have been raised and therefore that is most likely to be where my group consciousness lies. It's what feels right and works for me. Wicca was originally based on a Celtic-inspired pantheon.

The pantheon of Celtic Goddesses and Gods can seem confusing, maybe overwhelmingly so, at first. One has to remember that the Celtic tribes spread right across Europe from the eastern Mediterranean to Ireland, blending and fusing with other races as they went. You will therefore find the same aspects of many Goddesses and Gods being associated with different areas that the Celts covered and some even cross over into other religious belief systems from Greece, Rome and the Nordic races.

The Celtic Goddesses and Gods of Britain and Ireland themselves (forgetting the rest of Europe) can seem confusing enough – at least at first glance. Invasions throughout history have brought with them influences from the Saxons, Romans and Normans. Because of this the belief systems became intermingled, subverted, or at least blended. To add to the confusion, the priests of the Celts – the druids – gradually came to accept and were engulfed by a form of Celtic Christianity that was later to have been completely taken over by the Roman Church. The myths that seem to have survived better than most would appear to be those that survived in Ireland – not least of all because Ireland was subjected to fewer invasions than Britain, and therefore had fewer influences. These survived through some of the oldest pagan texts written down at a later stage (the pagan druids relied on preserving their myths through word of mouth). The best known Irish myths are based around the Tuatha De Dana – the people of Dana.[27] Many of the original Goddess and God figures were adopted by Christianity, such as the Goddess Brigid, who became Christianised as St. Brigit.

One of the best known allegorical stories, or set of stories, that has become Christianised from its pagan roots is clearly that of King Arthur and his 'knights' of the Round Table. These stories seem to have their roots in various parts of the Celtic domain including Wales, England, Cornwall and Brittany. These stories, particularly important to the British cultural identity for many, may well have been overlaid on top of truly historical figures and spiritually significant places such as Avalon (Glastonbury in Somerset) and Camelot (possible either nearby Cadbury or Tintagel). The story of the Holy Grail is one of finding the divine within. The Knights of the Round Table, like so many today, look for the Holy Grail in the material world, but fail to find it because they are looking in the wrong place. We all carry the Holy Grail with us all the time, we just have to learn where to look and discover how to grasp it with both hands.

FAITH IN THE POWERS OF NATURE

The Celts, it is said, laughed at the anthropomorphic statues and other images they found of Greek and Roman Gods. To the Celts, the Gods were inseparable from nature as that is where they were found – intrinsically intertwined with all living things as depicted by their well-known

---

[27] There is speculation that the 'people of Dana' were also active in Britain. Not only do many of the allegorical myths get reflected in British pagan myth albeit with different names of deities attached, but places such as London may well have originally been called 'Lan Dana' or 'Lan Dian' – the place of the people of Dana. A pagan altar to the Goddess Dana was found underneath the original St. Paul's Cathedral (burnt down in the fire of London in 1666). Part of the altar stone can be seen cast into the wall of a Chinese banking institution in the City of London.

knot-work designs. The Celtic Gods do not manifest themselves in mortal form, nor are they worshipped in such a form, but their aspects are seen in the land, throughout nature, and beyond in the energies and spirits of the Otherworld. The energies of the Goddess and God can be found in all things, be that the sun or moon, the land itself, as well as trees, herbs, stones, animals, and of course ourselves. The Celts were under no delusion about the powers that were available through the other planes of existence. They worshipped their Gods passionately not through some false delusion that those Gods would forgive all their sins however they treated the resources they were provided with. They did not worship some anthropomorphic form without understanding that those forms represented the powers of nature, the powers of the land and all life within the physical plane, the universe and the powers from above, as well as the energies from beyond the physical plane. Their stories were allegorical. They were under no delusion that those stories were allegorical and those who worked their magic fully understood the true meaning behind those allegorical teachings. They had faith in the natural powers that were abundant around them, and that are abundant around us still. Those powers are available to us, here and now, if only we can learn to have the same level of understanding – have the same level of faith.

To work with those energies, to truly make them work for us, they must be used according to natural laws that we must appreciate if those very same laws are not to rebound on us ourselves to adverse effect. Understanding the teachings of the Celts is one way of learning about those energies and appreciating the divine truth that the Goddess and God is within us all, as they are in all things – in everything we see and beyond. Reading, studying and meditating on what has been learnt is very important, as is getting out into the countryside and experiencing what has been studied.

Look after the Lady and the Lord at all levels and they will rise up in us and reward us; they will manifest themselves in us and through us. Work against the natural laws and we pay the penalty because that is the way nature works. That is why, if one wishes to follow the path of witchcraft, it is important to study the ways of our ancestors. It is not so that we can relive some romantic image of the past, but so that we can once again learn to work *with* nature and not destroy that which we rely on through worshipping the false gods of materialism that merely promise to destroy the natural resources the future existence of our own species needs to survive.

Whichever deity sets you choose to work with, and no matter which of the pagan belief systems you choose to follow, if indeed you do choose to go down that path at all, there is a common theme throughout. The

Goddesses and Gods fall into similar patterns whichever deity sets are used, which in itself signifies a common source. You may even choose to visualise those deities in a unique and modern way – the powers that be remain the same whatever name you choose to give them.

COMMON ASPECTS OF THE GODDESS AND GOD

The masculine god tends to fall into light and dark aspects, depicting Summer and Winter – the force that brings forth form as consort to the Goddess. The Goddess in this respect is seen as a nature Goddess who moves between the light and dark as different aspects of herself, but she is constant and never 'dies'. The God aspects are divided into two. There is the Holly King who is reborn at the height of the summer solstice, goes through a process of 'sacrifice' to bring fertility to the Goddess (the land) and finally gives way to his twin brother the Oak King when they overwhelm each other at the winter solstice. The Oak King also goes through a similar process of 'sacrifice' for the purposes of fertility. This is marked throughout the Sabbat ritual process as will be seen. The Oak King therefore represents the Earth God through the waxing half of the year and the Holly King throughout the waning half.

The Goddess is also represented in a triple aspect of Maiden, Mother and Crone, represented by the three phases of the Moon; this reflects her Earthly aspects of Spring, Summer and Winter[28]. There is also an Earth Mother Goddess and a God of the forest or of the animals (the Green Man). The Sun is also seen as a God figure, bringing the force of energy to the Earth Mother Goddess who uses this energy to provide for all living things.

Study of the various myths is something that I highly commend to you. There is not enough room in a book of this size to do them justice as they would require several volumes of their own and have been documented thoroughly by many other authors. (I have included a brief list of the British and Irish deity sets in the appendices of this book.)

The Celts, as well as having derivatives of the Earth Goddess, the Triple Goddess, the Sun God, etc. also had many goddess and god aspectations, often regional or tribal and associated with spiritual sites or with the warrior. Some of these are included in the appendices, others you will almost certainly discover if you continue your studies into the Celtic culture. There are several hundred of them in all, many of which are regional variations of similar aspects.

---

[28] The Celts originally divided their year into three seasons – Spring, Summer and Winter – rather than four.

Through study of these myths you will discover more about the way our ancestors saw their world, how closely they associated with their Otherworld (the land of 'Faery'[29]) and their Underworld. Whilst one need not associate various deity figures from the Celtic race in your work, it is quite possible that you will be drawn to these stories if you associate with the Celtic cultural group soul. As I have said before throughout this book – do what feels right to you and follow your own individual intuition.

You will also see how they used allegorical stories using Goddess and God figures to teach the process of initiation into the mysteries such as the story of the Goddess Cerridwen and a young man called Gwion. In this story, for instance, Gwion is given the task of stirring a potion created by his mother Cerridewen for her son. Whilst stirring the cauldron a drop of the magic potion splashes on to Gwion's finger which he sucks and gains the wisdom intended for Cerridwen's son. Annoyed by this, Cerridwen pursues Gwion throughout the land. In an effort to escape, Gwion becomes a shape-shifter. He first becomes a hare, and Cerridwen becomes a greyhound; then he becomes a salmon, which is pursued by Cerridwen who becomes an otter; then a bird, pursued by a falcon; then finally a piece of corn, pursued by a hen. As a hen, Cerridwen eventually finds Gwion and swallows the piece of corn. The Goddess then gives birth to Taliesin – Gwion reborn – who becomes a great bard. The story is one of initiation through the elements of earth (hare and greyhound), water (fish and otter), air (bird and falcon), and fire (corn and hen) which leads to the rebirth of the initiate as an enlightened bard in the form of Taliesin.

As a pagan we must learn to stir the cauldron of the Goddess and to become a witch we must learn to work with the elements of nature. By learning how to work with and master these energies we may then pass through the doors of initiation and become reborn as a witch and priestess or priest, to find the Goddess and God within and to allow them to work through us for the good of all.

Study of the pagan myths, the Celtic as well as those of the Saxon, Northern Tradition, Mithraic, Egyptian, and others is an exercise that can be very interesting and rewarding. However, it is well to remember that whilst history is important, especially the allegories hidden in the myths, it is only of any use if we apply what we have learnt to the present and the future. It is easy to become lost in a romantic revival of the past and forget to evolve what we have learnt into a modern context.

---

[29] The 'Gifts of Faery' are reflected in the tools representing the elements used in witchcraft, with but a slight variation.

15

BASIC CIRCLE CASTING

The following basic circle casting ritual is based on a Gardnerian Wiccan method which I have modified and modernised. It can be used in any ritual situation from worship at full or new moons and any of the major sabbats (or solar festivals) as well as initiations and magic workings. The worship or ritual is slotted in between the casting and opening ceremony. It is written here for a male and female (priest and priestess) couple, but can easily be adapted for the solitary witch or a full coven. Use it as a guide, and never be afraid to use your own words if you feel more comfortable with them. However, it is strongly advised that the essential elements are included and followed, whatever words you prefer to use.

The Circle helps to contain the power and focus the magical energy. A properly cast circle creates a sacred space that bridges the gap 'between the worlds' where magic can be worked on all levels. Stepping into a Circle that is properly prepared is to step into a space that spans the dimensions – a multidimensional reality broader than we generally perceive.

Whilst it is generally described as a 'Circle' and the work done 'between the worlds' is often described as 'Circle work' this is not an entirely accurate description. What you are actually casting, and it is important to remember this throughout the casting procedure, is a sphere. One draws a circle on the ground around the perimeter defined by the positions of the four quarters of North, South, East and West, but we visualise a sphere. The first thing we do is welcome the Goddess and God. What we are actually doing is opening up channels (I will not use the word invoke when referring to the Gods as this would be disrespectful)[30] to the Earth Goddess – the dark energies from below – and the Sun God – the light from above. Thus when the sphere is completely cast with the Guardians of the Quarters invoked we truly

---

[30] One 'invokes' the Guardians of the Elements because a witch is expected to master the Elements, but one 'invites' the Gods. Though 'master' is not meant as in the relationship of a master and slave, but more as in the mastery of a virtuoso over his instrument.

stand between the worlds. We stand in the centre of a place of balance between the four elements, as well as between the powers of light and darkness as the figure below depicts.

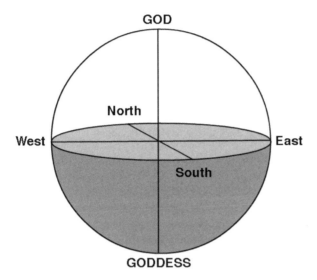

▲ *Figure 7 – The cast 'Circle'.*

All witches should be thoroughly conversant with circle casting techniques. It is not necessary for one to be a High Priestess or High Priest to cast a Circle, though certain ceremonies and rituals do require the presence of a High Priestess and High Priest. Within a Circle situation all female witches are referred as a Priestess and all male witches as a Priest, an honour conferred on to each witch from their first initiation.

All movements within the Circle should be deosil (pronounced 'jeshel', i.e. clockwise, the way the sun moves) except when clearing the Circle which is performed widdershins (anti-clockwise).

You will need to learn how to draw a pentacle. This is drawn in a different way for each of the four quarters. Referring to the diagram below you will see that each of the points of the pentacle relate to one of the four elements of Earth, Air, Fire and Water, with the uppermost point relating to what is seen as the fifth element of Spirit.

During the Circle casting one will need to invoke the elements in turn. This is done by drawing a pentagram in the air with the blade of the athame. There is a different way of drawing each element, and this obviously needs to be memorised. With each of the elements of earth, air, fire and water one starts by drawing the first line towards the point representing that element, then moving around the pentagram (this does not apply to the pentagram for the element of spirit). There is then one final stroke from that point from which one started, to the point representing the element in question and as you draw this last stroke, visualise and feel the presence of that element arriving. A banishing pentacle is the same in reverse, i.e. starting at the point representing the element and going back the way you came with the final stroke away from that element you visualise and feel the presence of that element departing. However, the direction in which one invokes the elements is different for the active elements of fire and water, and the passive elements of earth and air. For the passive elements one moves around the pentagram anti-clockwise (i.e. for air the first stroke would be from water to air); for the active elements one moves around the penta-gram clockwise (i.e. for fire the first stroke would be from spirit to fire).

▲ *Figure 8 – The Elements on the Pentagram.*

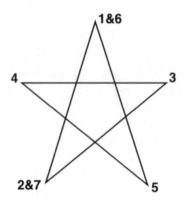

▲ *Figure 9 – Invoking Pentagram of the Earth Element.*

112

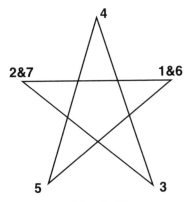

▲ *Figure 10 – Invoking Pentagram of the Air Element.*

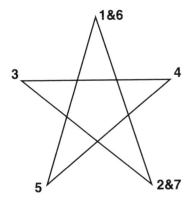

▲ *Figure 11 – Invoking Pentagram of the Fire Element.*

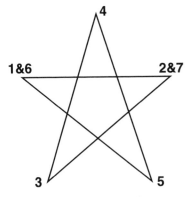

▲ *Figure 12 – Invoking Pentagram of the Water Element.*

In the basic circle casting described below, it will not be necessary to draw an invoking pentagram for the element of spirit. However, when this is used there are two forms of drawing the pentagram for such a purpose; one for invoking an active spirit and another for invoking a passive spirit

An active invoking pentagram for spirit begins at the active element of fire with the first stroke towards air, then moving around the pentagram to finish at fire. A passive invoking pentagram for spirit begins at earth with the first stroke towards water. As before, once invoked the spirit will be eventually banished by drawing the pentagram in reverse with the final stroke extended and emphasised with the appropriate visualisation. Ensure that this is done thoroughly and properly.

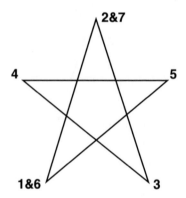

▲ *Figure 13 – Invoking Pentagram of the Spirit Element (Active).*

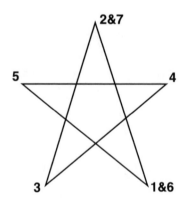

▲ *Figure 14 – Invoking Pentagram of the Spirit Element (Passive).*

PREPARATION

Have all the tools ready for the ritual. If you are working indoors make sure the space you are using is cleaned and hoovered (or swept). If working outdoors, choose a place that is private, quiet, where the ground is reasonably flat and free of thistles and stinging nettles that would be painful when trod on with naked feet. If you are lucky enough to have access to a garden that is not overlooked by prying eyes it would be a good idea to keep a space for your temple. It could be marked permanently with stones and an altar table of stone or wood. One could even surround such a garden temple with flowering plants and trees in the appropriate quarters according to their various correspondences.

The size of the Circle can be large or small. Nine feet in diameter is traditional in a coven though I find this far too small, eighteen feet would be better for a large ceremony. It can be delineated with a cord, drawn, or just visualised. The size of the Circle is not of vital importance. The important thing is to ensure it is large enough for the number of people using it to move around without bumping into each constantly, but not so big as to cause it a problem containing the visualisation and energy.

As a general rule, if working as Priestess and Priest, the Priestess is in overall charge of proceedings.

The four quarters, or 'watchtowers', are marked with candles. Coloured candles are ideal, but any will do. A Wiccan circle is generally marked with coloured candles as follows:

NORTH – GREEN – EARTH
EAST – YELLOW – AIR
SOUTH – RED – FIRE
WEST – BLUE – WATER

However, I often work with and prefer what would appear to be more genuine Celtic correspondences which are:

NORTH – BLACK (for midnight) – EARTH
EAST – RED (symbolising the rising sun) – AIR
SOUTH – WHITE (for the brightness of the midday sun) – FIRE
WEST – GREY (twilight) – WATER

As with most things the choice is yours and it is best to follow what feels most right for you at the time. Green, yellow, red and blue would appear to correspond to the elemental correspondences better, though black, red, white and grey better with the course of the Sun.

The altar should normally be placed in the middle of the Circle facing North or East but can be placed on the Northern edge if more space is required. A coffee table can be used for the altar, although a suitably sized and shaped log would be better, plastic and any other man-made materials should be avoided where possible as they don't conduct the energies too well if at all. An altar cloth is usually used, the colour being one suitable to the occasion. All the tools, and anything else required for the work, should be placed on the altar. There would normally be a central altar candle, with a candle for the Goddess on the left and one for the God on the right towards the rear. Tapers are useful for lighting the candles if you have them.

Review what work is going to be undertaken before casting the circle.

Wear what feels comfortable or appropriate (ordinary clothes, robes or naked). Wear appropriate jewellery. I prefer to keep a number of jewellery items that I use exclusively for when I dress for such occasions so that I feel I am dressing up for a special occasion, for that is what I am doing.

Have a bath, or at least wash, before the ceremony. A herbal bath is particularly good. The addition of salt to the bath helps to properly cleanse the body and spirit. The phrase 'Cleanliness is next to Godliness' is one entirely appropriate within Wicca, and one that should be particu-larly be borne in mind before Circle work. Dirt interferes with our energy flow and also potentially shows disrespect for the divine energies that we intend to work with.

Once the Circle has been cast, stay within the boundary if possible. If you have to leave – excuse yourself and apologise to the Goddess and God, make a gateway at the North-Eastern edge with the athame and return as soon as possible. To make a gateway the circle must be cut with the athame three times and sealed afterwards. To seal the Circle on entering or leaving a pentagram is drawn with the athame. If you need to leave for any length of time – end the ritual and close the Circle.

The Circle can be formed starting from the North or the East. Start from the North if the intended work is of an earthly matter, from the East if it is more spiritual.

As I have said before, this ritual is designed for two people, in this case a High Priestess and High Priest. It can easily be adapted for anything from a solitary witch to a full coven. The roles can equally be undertaken by a Priestess and Priest who have not been initiated to the third degree, though regard must be given to the type of work or ceremony which is undertaken within the Circle as some of them, such as a Handfasting, require witches of the third degree.

There are some elements that sometimes need to be slotted into the ritual on occasions. For instance, it is quite common for the High Priest to 'draw down the moon' into the High Priestess, and for the High Priestess to draw down the Sun into the High Priest. This is an element of ritual work that invokes the Goddess and God into the High Priestess and High Priest for the duration of the work. This rituals are detailed in the next chapter. Those two invocations, in particular, are best done outside within sight of the Sun or Moon (sunset is best for the Sun, and Full Moon for the Moon). If you are not having the Circle outside, it can be performed outside either by doing it before casting the Circle, or by cutting a gateway during the Circle in order to leave. They can be done inside, within the Circle using visualisation techniques though it takes far less effort and is often far more effective if undertaken with the Sun or Moon before you.

CASTING THE CIRCLE

High Priest lights the central altar candle which represents the One divine source that existed before creation. High Priest lights charcoal in the censer (adding incense when alight) or incense sticks from the altar candle. High Priest and High Priestess stand before the altar, High Priestess on the left.

High Priestess – "The circle is about to be cast. We stand within the circle to greet the Goddess and the God."

High Priestess goes to the North of the circle with athame in hand. She lowers her athame and walks around the boundary of the circle visualising a light blue light emanating from the point and forming the circle/temple boundary. As she passes the Eastern quarter and continues walking she says:

"I draw this circle in the presence of the Goddess and of the God so that they may bless us. This is the boundary of the circle. Only peace and love may enter and leave."

High Priestess lights the Goddess candle from the central altar candle. High Priest lights the God candle.

High Priestess place the point of her athame in the salt and says – "Salt is life and purifies. I bless this salt for use within this circle in the names of the Goddess and the God."

She picks up the salt bowl and drop three portions into the water. She replaces the salt bowl and stirs the water deosil three times with the point of her athame.[31] As she does this she says – "Let the salt purify this water so that it too may be blessed for use in this circle. In the names of the Goddess and of the God I consecrate and cleanse this water."

---

[31] The High Priestess combines the salt (representing Earth) and water for the same reasons as above.

High Priestess picks up the bowl of salted water and moves around the circle, from the East to the East, sprinkling it as she goes.

High Priest picks up the censer (ensuring incense is still flowing) or incense sticks and follows the High Priestess around the circle.[32]

The circle has now effectively been drawn three times. Once using spirit (using the athame), once using water and salt, and once using the incense (Earth, Air, Fire and Water).

High Priestess takes the altar candle, or lights a taper from the candle. High Priest takes up his athame and moves to stand before the candle marking the Eastern quarter. High Priestess follows him with candle and her athame in hand.

High Priest [33] – "Watchers of the East, Guardians of Air, I summon, stir and call you to attend this rite and guard our circle."

High Priestess lights the Eastern candle as the High Priest draws an invoking pentagram for Air above the candle. As they do this they both visualise and sense the element of Air arriving from the East.

High Priest lowers athame and moves to the candle marking the Southern quarter with High Priestess following.

High Priest – "Watchers of the South, Guardians of Fire, I summon, stir and call you to attend this rite and guard our circle."

High Priestess lights the Southern candle as the High Priest draws an invoking pentagram for Fire above the candle. As they do this they both visualise and sense the element of Fire arriving from the South.

High Priest lowers athame. High Priestess hands candle to High Priest and they both move to stand before the candle marking the Western quarter.

High Priestess – "Watchers of the West, Guardians of Water, I summon, stir and call you to attend this rite and guard our circle."

High Priest lights the Western candle as the High Priestess draws an invoking pentagram for Water above the candle. As they do this they both visualise and sense the element of Water arriving from the West.

High Priestess lowers athame and both move to stand before the candle marking the Northern quarter.

High Priestess – "Watchers of the North, Guardians of Earth, I summon, stir and call you to attend this rite and guard our circle."

---

[32] The High Priest takes the burning incense, representing fire and air as they correspond to the masculine.

[33] The High Priest invokes the Eastern and Southern quarters as Air and Fire correspond to the masculine; the High Priestess invokes the Western and Northern quarters as Water and Earth correspond to the feminine.

High Priest lights the Northern candle as the High Priestess draws an invoking pentagram for Earth above the candle. As they do this they both visualise and sense the element of Earth arriving from the North.

Both High Priest and High Priestess move deosil around the circle to stand as before in front of the altar. NB: At this point, if working with others, the High Priest would move to a position at the North-East of the Circle and open a gateway to allow the others, who would have been waiting outside the Circle, to enter. To open a gateway the High Priest uses his athame and 'cuts' a line drawing back and forth three times, holding the athame in position whilst those outside enter, then passes an athame back three times the other way to seal the circle. He then stands back and draws a standard banishing pentagram where the gateway was cut.

High Priestess picks up her athame and holding it aloft in both hands says – "The Circle is now formed, consecrated and sealed with the Mighty Ones called from the quarters. We stand between the worlds to welcome the Lady and Lord, Goddess and God."

High Priest uses the wand to draw the sign of infinity (an 8 lying on its side) over the altar. This signifies that we are now working between the worlds.

The High Priestess takes the anointing oil and uses it to draw a solar (or Celtic) cross[34] on the forehead of the High Priest saying – "I consecrate you in the names of the Goddess and the God in this, their circle." The High Priest then takes the anointing oil and consecrates the High Priestess using the same words. If there are others in the Circle, then the High Priestess consecrates them all with the oil in the same fashion.

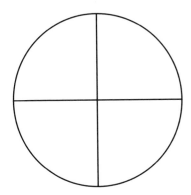

▲ *Figure 15 – The Solar Cross.*

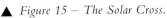

[34] To draw a Solar Cross, draw the circle first (deosil) then draw the upright line followed by the horizontal line.

High Priestess pours a little wine[35] into the Chalice then holds it in two hands before her chest. High Priest picks up his athame and holds it point down in two hands above the wine and slowly dips it into the Chalice[36] saying — "I bless and consecrate this wine in the name of the Goddess and God."

High Priest removes Athame from wine and replaces it on the altar. High Priestess pours a small amount of wine into the water (if indoors, or on to the earth if outside). This is the first libation offered to the Goddess. She then holds the chalice up to the lips of the High Priest and allows him to sip the wine. The High Priest then takes the chalice and holds it to the lips of his High Priestess for her to take a sip. If there are others in the Circle then the High Priest or High Priestess takes the wine around the Circle for each to take a sip.

This ends the standard Circle Casting procedure. At this point you continue with whatever ceremony, magic or ritual work you decided to undertake beforehand.

CLOSING THE CIRCLE

When all is finished, the High Priestess holds her athame in her power hand level over the altar and says — "Lord and Lady — God and Goddess — We have been blessed by you sharing this time with us, watching and guarding us, and guiding us here and in all things. We came in love — and depart in love."

High Priestess raises her athame in a salute and says — "Love is the law and love is the bond. Merry did we meet, merry do we part, and merry will we meet again."

High Priestess kisses the flat of the blade.

High Priest and High Priestess go to the candle at the Northern quarter. High Priestess holds athame aloft and says — "Watchers of the North, Guardians of Earth, we thank you for attending this rite and guarding this Circle and ask for your blessings as you depart. Hail and farewell."

High Priestess draws banishing pentagram of Earth in the air as the High Priest snubs out the candle.

High Priest and High Priestess go to the candle at the Western quarter. High Priestess holds athame aloft and says — "Watchers of the

---

[35] Red wine is usually used as it represents the blood of the Goddess.

[36] The Chalice represents the womb of the Goddess and the wine her blood. The Athame in this instance represents the spirit and phallus of the God. It is a minor form of the Great Rite.

West, Guardians of Water, we thank you for attending this rite and guarding this Circle and ask for your blessings as you depart. Hail and farewell."

High Priestess draws banishing pentagram of Water in the air as the High Priest snubs out the candle.

High Priest and High Priestess go to the candle at the Southern quarter. High Priest holds athame aloft and says – "Watchers of the South, Guardians of Fire, we thank you for attending this rite and guarding this Circle and ask for your blessings as you depart. Hail and farewell."

High Priest draws banishing pentagram of Fire in the air as the High Priestess snubs out the candle.

High Priest and High Priestess go to the candle at the Eastern quarter with athames. High Priest holds athame aloft and says – "Watchers of the East, Guardians of Air, we thank you for attending this rite and guarding this Circle and ask for your blessings as you depart. Hail and farewell."

High Priest draws banishing pentagram of Air in the air as the High Priestess snubs out the candle. Both return to altar.

High Priestess – "Powers of the visible and invisible, depart in peace. You aid us in our work, whisper in our minds and bless us. There is harmony between us. The circle is cleared."

High Priestess takes her athame again to the East, points down and walks widdershins (anti-clockwise) around the circle back to the East. As she goes she envisages the blue light drawing back into the athame. On reaching the East again she says – "The Circle is open yet the Circle remains as the power is drawn back into me." She holds the point of her Athame to her forehead and feels the energy flow back into her mind.

All participants should now ensure that they are thoroughly grounded.

16

ESBATS

The monthly cycle of the Moon and the changing energies that are associated with it are used considerably in witchcraft, as are the annual cycles of the Sun (see *Sabbats*). It should not be underestimated or forgotten how the planetary bodies affect us on Earth in many ways from our general character at birth through to the energies that affect us day to day and even hour to hour in subtle (and often not so subtle) ways. It is also necessary to take into account the greater pattern of the aeons such as the Pisces and Aquarian ages especially at the turn of the year 2000 CE where we are gradually moving from the former to the latter[37]. Astrology is a subject that should be carefully studied by any witch worth their salt and few indeed would be found without an ephemeris as an essential element of their armoury.[38]

The Moon is so close to the Earth that it drastically affects tides causing a pull that can lift enormous bodies of water. It is no wonder then that those energies also profoundly affect us as well especially when we consider that our bodies consist largely of water.

A Celtic year, adopted by the Druids, was divided into 13 months (or 'moonths') corresponding to the 13 Full Moons in a year (see appendices).

Women especially will feel closely associated with the Moon. The Moon with its 29 day progression corresponds with the female menstrual cycle and represents in most pagan belief systems the Goddess albeit under

---

[37] There is much speculation over how long an Age lasts, as well as how long it takes to complete the transition from one to the other. It would appear to be around 2,000 years which would account for the growing and changing spiritual values that are evident in our time towards Aquarian values, and the male dominated and blinkered approach of the previous Piscean Age that started around the time Christianity began.

[38] Astrology is a subject on which there are many vast and useful volumes to study. There is not enough room in this book to give the subject more than a brief mention, but it is recommended that further reading is sought.

different names[39]. Priestesses of the Craft particularly may find that as they tune into the Moon and work with her energies that their own menstrual cycle begins to match that of this heavenly progression. However, male witches should also seek to balance themselves using the lunar cycle. It is all part of finding the balance within to worship both the solar cycle and the lunar cycle. I also feel strongly, for the same reason, that esbats should also be held to mark the dark moon as well, for the same reason, but more of that later.

In witchcraft, the Celtic tradition in particular, as well as other spiritual paths, the Moon is represented by a triplicity of Goddesses – maiden, mother and crone – that mark her phases. The waxing moon (the period following the New Moon and leading up to the Full) represents the maiden aspect. The Full Moon represents the Goddess in her mother aspect. The waning Moon (following the Full Moon and up to the Dark Moon) represents the Goddess in her crone aspect. There are many anthropomorphic triplicity sets of Goddesses even within the Celtic traditions (see appendices for details).

In magic, the waxing Moon is used for work or spells that involve growth as the pull is increasing, the Full Moon for fertility and power, the waning Moon for work involving getting rid of negativity and other darker matters. Witches tend to hold their celebrations, and do much of their work, under the Full Moon because the Goddess is seen in her full glory and because the Moon is then offering its strongest pull (its greatest power) at this time. The pull of the Full Moon can have a tremendous effect, not just on the oceans, but on living things including plants and animals. It is believed, and there is some evidence to back it up, that those of us who are unbalanced can feel particularly so under the influence of a Full Moon; the word 'lunatic' comes from this effect.

Farmers of old, and many of this modern age (especially those in the organic movement), plant and harvest their crops for best results according to the Moon's cycle. Crops that grow above ground are planted during the waxing cycle to give them the head start the Moon's pull provides, whilst root crops tend to be planted during a waning Moon. Witches and others interested in herbalism know that herbs picked during the full moon phase contain a great deal more energy than at other times. This is because the sap and the associated energy rises in the plant during that time.

Witches, whether they work in a group (coven) or solitary tend to work at the Full Moon, and sometimes at the Dark Moon. This is, in part,

---

[39] The Moon is sometimes seen as masculine and the Sun feminine as in the Northern Tradition and some elements of the Celtic tribes throughout history. The Goddess Grainne (for instance) who gives her name to the powerful Irish site of Newgrange is a solar deity.

an act of worship, holding the Goddess in awe and respect, but also times when working certain forms of magic are most appropriate. These meetings tend to be known in the modern Craft as Esbats[40].

DRAWING DOWN THE MOON

This is a ritual element that should ideally be part of a Circle ceremony or ritual. It is best done outside under the Full Moon. The intention is to draw down the energy of the moon, in other words to invoke the Goddess, into the Priestess and is conducted by the Priest. I find that this works quite effectively with two partners who are used to working together without actually using any words. As one is directing energies, words can be a distraction, but for purposes of times when words are desired I include them in the following.

The Priestess stands in front of the Priest either facing the moon or facing the Priest. The Priest can use his athame or just his hands. The Priest positions himself so that the Priestess is standing about nine feet in front of him between him and the moon above. Both stand for a few moments to attune with the moon and concentrate on the Goddess image with which she corresponds.

If using his hands the Priest holds his hands aloft with finger tips joined in such a way that the moon is embraced within his arms. Pulling on the energy of the moon he gradually brings his arms down, separating his fingers and drawing the moon's energy into the Priestess's aura. He should pull this energy completely around her and seal it beneath her feet. If conducted properly, the Priestess will feel the change in energy as the Priest completes this short ritual.

If using an athame, the Priest starts by holding the athame in both hands, arms straight in front of his head. He will find that he can position the athame in such a way that the moon appears to be inside the blade of the athame. He holds this position for a moment concentrating on drawing in the moon's energy, then completes a drawing movement around (and mentally into) the Priestess's aura as before.

Whilst drawing down the moon the following words can be used if desired.

---

[40] 'Esbat' is a term that appears to have been derived by Dr Margaret Murray from the French *s'essbattre*, which means to frolic. The word does appear in the records of a 16th century witch trial though there seems little evidence that witches and/or druids of the past in Celtic lands used the term. Whether it is a word of genuine antiquity, or one that has been adopted through the introduction of Wicca is of no great consequence. I suggest you use the term if you feel comfortable with it, or not as the case may be.

"Bright Lady of the night sky,
who represents our beautiful Goddess,
and who reflects tonight,
the light of our God,
as they work together in harmony,
I draw down your energy into this,
My Priestess in your name and honour".

THE FIVE-FOLD KISS

The five-fold kiss is normally used by the Priest after drawing down the moon into the Priestess and at other times when a blessing is called upon. It is occasionally used by a Priestess to bless the Priest in a similar fashion for the same reason. Priest kneels before the Priestess as she stands with her arms folded across her chest. When the Priest reaches the womb she opens her arms wide to the blessing position with hands facing forward and skywards, and elbows at right angles. The Priest kisses her lightly on the right foot, the left foot, the right knee, the left knee, the womb (above the phallus if the Priestess is giving the blessing), the right breast, the left breast and finally the lips. As they kiss they embrace length to length with their feet touching each others. Whilst doing this the Priest says:

"Blessed be your feet, that brought you to this place.
Blessed be your knees that shall kneel at the sacred altar.
Blessed be your womb (phallus) without which we should not be.
Blessed be your breasts formed in beauty (strength).
Blessed be your lips that shall utter the Sacred Names of our Lady
and Lord."

The Priest then takes a step back and kneels with his hands stretched out wide, and bows to the Priestess touching his head against the floor to honour the Goddess.

CHARGE OF THE GREAT GODDESS

The following is the Charge of the Great Goddess based on the first known published version by Charles Leyland in 1899 and thought to have been provided to him from a group of practising witches in Italy. There is some doubt about the source, however, this is not important as far as I am concerned; wherever it came from it is beautifully appropriate and serves the purpose more than well. Several versions have since been published by people such as Doreen Valiente, Starhawk and the Farrars. This is my version. The Charge is generally included near the beginning of a Full Moon Esbat ritual.

Listen to the words of the Great Goddess,
Who throughout time has been known by many names.

Assemble in a sacred place of your own making when the Moon is full,
and any other time you have need of My aid.
Know that My love will make you free,
for nobody can prevent your worship of Me in your mind and your heart.
Listen well when you worship,
and I will teach you the deep mysteries, ancient and powerful.
I require no sacrifices or pain, for I am the Mother of all things,
the Creatress who made you out of My love,
and the One who endures through all time.

I am the beauty of the Earth, the green of growing things.
I am the white Moon whose light is full among the stars and soft upon the Earth.
From Me all things are born, to Me all things, in their seasons return.
Let my worship be in your hearts, for all acts of love and pleasure are My rituals.
You see Me in the love of man and woman, the love of parent and child.
I stand beside you always, whispering soft words of wisdom and guidance.
You need only listen.

All seekers of the Mysteries must come to Me,
for I am the True Source, the Keeper of the Cauldron.
All who seek to know Me, know this.
All your seeking and yearning will be in vain unless you understand the Mystery
that if what you seek is not found within, you will never find it without.
For behold, I have been with you from the beginning,
and I will gather you to my breast at the end.

Blessed Be.

DRAWING DOWN THE SUN

This is the complementary ritual to the drawing down of the Moon and is conducted by the Priestess for the Priest. Its intention is to draw down the energy of the Sun, thus invoking the God, into the Priest. Again I find it works well with two partners who are used to working together to conduct it without words.

The best time to choose is around sunset, though it can be done at anytime. The ritual is conducted in a similar way to that above, with the roles reversed and the Priestess using the athame instead of the Priest. However, whilst it is safe to stare at the Moon, it is not a good idea to stare directly into the Sun, therefore I would suggest that at this point both the Priest and Priestess face the Sun with eyes closed and feel its energy.

DARK MOON

As I said earlier, I feel strongly that esbats should also mark the dark cycle of the moon. Far too many witches only ever work with the full moon, the Goddess in her light cycle, and deny the darkness. This can lead to imbalance. Balance is an essential element within Wicca; balance between Goddess and God, feminine and masculine, dark and light. Our own culture has, for too long, recognised and worked with only the light aspects which I consider to be a considerable error. If we work only with the light then we end up with our head in the clouds without them being firmly rooted on the ground. If we work entirely with the dark we end up being miserable and destroying everything around us that has any real value.

Casting a circle under the dark moon cycle we can address our darker inner feelings that are so often suppressed by using this time to meditate. Whether we acknowledge it or not, we all have a dark side to our nature. Our Western culture, and especially the Christian Church, tends to expect us to hide this element within ourselves. I would encourage all of you to look within yourselves, bring that dark side of yourselves to the surface and find a reasonable way of expressing it openly. In Jungian terms the dark aspects include our shadow Self. If we are to become complete and fully developed individuals in touch with our High Selves then we need to acknowledge the 'shadow' and incorporate it fully into our lives rather than denying it, which is what far too many people do. It is not an easy process, but one that must be tackled if one is to progress fully in the self-development process.

The following charges are particularly effective if used before a meditation during a dark moon Circle.

CHARGE OF THE DARK GODDESS[41]

Hear now, the words of the Dark Goddess,
who comes forth from her cavern of trickling waters and baying hounds.
I am the eternal soul, the dark maiden, the mother of night, and the patron of witches.
Fear not my power, for I am justice, the keeper of the keys, and the bearer of ancient wisdom.

---

[41] With kind permission of Lady Azure Ra, High Priestess of the Flamedancer Circle, Fort Lauderdale, Florida.

I come to you during the dark of the moon, that I may lead as your soul's mirror.
My vision spans all directions, as I walk the endless crossed roads in darkness.
I travel between the worlds, yours and mine.
My children, that I may guide you through the shadows of the underworld.

As I stand on the edge of sanity, cloaked, veiled, with glowing eyes and a
blazing torch.
My appearance is intense, but you shall learn, my fearful ones,
that it is I who brings you fairness and resolution.
It is I who protects you, my suffered children of the Earth.
It is I who heals your wounds and makes you strong.
It is I, Queen of the Underworld, who charges you by the light of my love,
and responds to your call in the winter when the night is still.

CHARGE OF THE DARK GOD

I am the shadow in the bright day;
I am the reminder of mortality at the height of living.
I am the never ending veil of night where the Star Goddess dances.
I am the death that must be so that life may continue,
for behold, Life is immortal because the living must die.
I am the strength that protects, that limits;
I am the power that says no, and no further, and that is enough.
I am the things that cannot be spoken of,
and I am the laughter at the edge of death.
Come with me into the warm unfolding dark;
feel my caresses in the hands, in the mouth,
in the body of one you love, and be transformed.
Gather in the moonless night and speak in unknown tongues;
and the Dark Mother and I will listen.
Sing out and cry out, and the power will be yours to wield.
Blow me a kiss when the sky is dark, and I will smile,
but no kiss return; for my kiss is the final one for all mortal flesh.

THE GREAT RITE

The Great Rite is an element of ceremonial work that is used on many occasions. I include it here rather than reproducing it several times during the chapters on sabbats and other rituals. The Great Rite represents the divine union between the Goddess and the God. As such it can take one of two forms. Either a symbolic rite utilising the chalice and the athame, or it can be performed in actuality if in private and your partner is your normal sexual partner and used to working with you. Whether it be symbolic or actual, the Great Rite clearly requires two, one of each gender.

Priest and Priestess move to centre of circle, she with her back to the altar, and he with his back to the South.

Priestess lays herself on the ground, hips in centre of circle, head to altar, arms and legs outstretched to form the pentacle.

Priest fetches a veil and lays it over her, covering from breasts to knees. He kneels facing her with his knees at her feet. He takes out his athame and takes hold of the chalice.

Priest delivers the invocation

"Goddess of the Stars and of the Earth,
In your womb all things grow,
And from your womb all things enter life,
And to you all things return.
We are of you, as you are of us.
This Woman before me is your Priestess,
An Earthly representation of you,
And we place her womb in the centre of our Circle,
As our great altar before which we worship.
This is as things should be,
In honour of you our Goddess who we love and adore.
That which we love and adore we also invoke.
Queen of the Stars, Mother of all, Jewel of light,
Who transcends all time and space,
By seed and root, and stem and bud,
Leaf and flower and fruit, we invoke you,
Into this your Priestess."

Priest removes the veil.

Priestess rises and kneels facing her Priest taking the chalice from him.

Priest continues . . .

"Altar of mysteries manifest,
The sacred Circle's secret point.
I sign you as of old,
With my lips anoint you."

The Priest than kisses the Priestess on her right foot, womb, left foot, right knee, left knee, right foot and finally on her womb. This represents the active pentagram of the spirit.

The Priestess holds up the chalice.

If the Rite is symbolic then the High Priest lowers the point of his athame into the wine. Both use both hands for this. If the Rite is actual then the Priest lays on top of the Priestess guiding his phallus into her vagina.

Priest continues:

"Here where the lance and grail unite,
Where the Goddess meets the God,
Uniting as One within you,
Do we understand the Great Mystery."

Priest puts his athame on the altar then places both hands around the chalice. He kisses her, she sips the wine; she kisses him, he sips the wine. The chalice is then replaced on the altar.

THE BLESSING OF CAKES AND WINE

The blessing of the cakes and wine follow most of the ceremonies just before the Circle is closed. The wine should be red as it represents the blood of the Goddess, the cakes represent her body and help the important grounding process necessary at the end of any work. To bless the wine, the Priest kneels before the Priestess and holds up the Chalice that has been filled with wine. He takes his athame and lowers it into the Chalice saying:

"I consecrate this wine in the names of the Lady and Lord, Goddess and God."

The Priest then puts down his athame and takes the Chalice and offers it to the lips of the Priestess who takes a sip. The Priestess then takes the Chalice and offers it to the Priest, who also takes a sip. The wine is then taken around to everyone else in the Circle – man to woman, woman to man – so that everyone has taken a sip. Once the Circle has been closed, the Chalice remains in circulation whilst any informal chat takes place. There is no need to re-consecrate the wine if the Chalice is refilled.

To bless the cakes, the Priest kneels before the Priestess holding up the plate. She draws an invoking pentagram of Earth over the cakes saying:

"I consecrate these cakes in the names of the Lady and Lord, Goddess and God. May they bring us health, wealth, joy and peace and fill us all with love and happiness."

The cakes are then passed around the Circle in the same way as the wine. The cakes, being made from corn, represent the body of the Goddess, and the wine, initially pressed from grapes, represents her blood. Christians adopted a similar element to this in their rituals as they did with many of the pagan ways.

SABBAT CAKE RECIPE

Four ounces of butter
Two eggs
One tablespoon of honey
Two tablespoons of cream
Six ounces of wholemeal flour
Large pinch of cinnamon

Cream the butter with a fork, then add the eggs, honey and cream and beat. Fold in the flour and cinnamon. Traditionally they are made into crescent moon shapes. Bake in an oven at around 180 degrees Centigrade for about ten minutes. When they have cooled, finish them with a sprinkling of cinnamon.

PUTTING AN ESBAT RITUAL TOGETHER

Throughout this book I have emphasised how important it is that Wicca remains an individualistic path. Rituals, as much as anything else, should be constructed by yourselves and you should feel free and confident to use the words provided here, adapt them as you feel the need, or completely re-write your own as you please.

I have provided elements of ritual that can be pieced together in building block form to suit your needs and circumstances. Below I show how a typical Full Moon Esbat ritual might be put together using the elements in this book. The table on the left shows a ritual suitable and possible for someone working alone, the additions on the right could be added along with those elements on the left if working as a couple or group.

Solitary	**Additions for couple or group**
Cast Circle (Basic Circle Casting)	
	Drawing Down the Moon
	Five-fold kiss
Charge of the Great Goddess	
Magic, meditation work, etc	
	Great Rite
Cakes and Wine	
Close Circle (Basic Circle Casting)	

If putting a Dark Moon ritual together I would suggest that most of the above formula would be used, but with the Charge of the Dark Goddess substituted for the Charge of the Great Goddess and the removal of the Great Rite. I suggest this as the Great Rite is the divine union between the Goddess and God, where the Goddess is seen in her full triple aspectation, and during a Dark Moon one is working with only one aspect of the Goddess.

17

SABBATS – THE WHEEL OF THE YEAR

The thirteen Esbat celebrations in a year mark the monthly lunar cycle and this is an important element within the Wiccan path. Equally important are the eight Sabbat celebrations that mark the annual solar cycle. These eight Sabbats fall into two categories – the Greater Sabbats (Samhain, Imbolg, Beltane and Lughnasadh); and the Lesser Sabbats (the equinoxes and solstices given the names of Yule, Ostara, Comhain and Mabon).

A Celtic day runs from the time the sun sets, after all that is the end of the day, therefore the Greater Sabbat celebrations generally begin on what we would these days consider to be the evening before, as soon as the sun has set (i.e. Beltane celebrations start at sunset on 30th April). The Celtic year starts and finishes with Samhain[42] for much the same reason that a day starts and finishes at sunset. In terms of the solar year, having passed the autumn equinox and the daylight getting shorter and shorter, Samhain would be the equivalent of the sunset. Yule, soon after which the Christian calendar dictates the new year to begin, is the equivalent of midnight.

The traditional Gardnerian Sabbat ritual texts (devised by Gerald Gardner and Doreen Valiente) draw much of there logic from J.G. Frazier's work in a book entitled *The Golden Bough* and Robert Graves's work in his book *The White Goddess* with some other elements borrowed from authors such as Rudyard Kipling. Frazier's research for *The Golden Bough* established the concept of pagan sacrifices (more often the monarch) being used to ensure fertility of the land and to ensure the continuation of the solar cycle. Much of Frazier's work has been used to justify modern analogies within the pagan revivals as a way of including 'genuine' pagan elements that would have been included in times past. Frazier's own driving force would appear to have been more anti-Christian than pro-pagan. The traditional Wiccan texts for the Sabbats divide the

---

[42] Pronounced 'Sow-een' and otherwise know as Halloween or (in Christian terminology) All Hallows Eve.

solar year into two parts ruled by the 'Oak King' who is reborn at Yule taking over from the 'Holly King'. The Oak King rules from Yule to Comhain (the midsummer solstice) where the two kings battle it out and the Holly King takes over to rule until Yule. To add to what some may see as a confusion, each king is subject to a sacrifice and resurrection (through mating with the ever-living Goddess in her various guises) between each cycle at Beltane, Lughnasadh or Samhain (traditions vary). As far as I am concerned, these texts offer a reasonable analogy of the solar year and the relationship between the Goddess elements and the God elements. I have included some elements of these texts, along with variations of my own, in the suggestions for your own celebrations and rituals. The important thing is that we mark the solar year sinking to its lowest at Yule (the winter solstice) waxing in strength to Comhain (the midsummer solstice) and then waning again to start the process again at Yule. We use these energies in much the same way as we use the waxing and waning cycles of the moon and often (in magical work) in conjunction with those cycles. It is also important that the rituals you devise mark the relevance of those cycles to the fertility of the Earth, helping to germinate the seed in spring, coming to full flower in summer, fruit and harvest as we approach autumn and decay ready for rebirth as we approach winter.

Devising your own rituals within a broad pagan framework is part of the work of tuning in with nature. I encourage you all to use the standard Gardnerian texts as they are presented to you; take elements from them from which to devise your own; use the framework that I am providing within these pages to devise your own texts, or write your own totally from scratch. As I have said before, it is what feels right to you that is vital. Follow your own instincts and one shall not

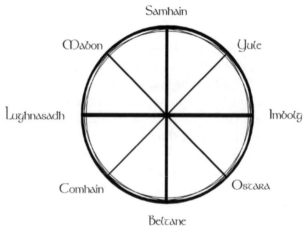

▲ *Figure 16 – The Wheel of the Year.*

go far wrong. Wicca has always been seen as a path in which dogma has little to play, and rightly so. It has also been firmly acknowledged that the texts need to change with the times in order to maintain there relevance. In the relatively short period from when Wicca was first presented to the outside world by Gardner in the 1950s, the scale of the environmental challenges facing our Earth Goddess has changed significantly. As we progress through the 21st Century we need to keep these challenges at the forefront of our mind and do everything within our power to meet those challenges. Being flexible and moving with the times is therefore an essential element if we are to be successful.

SAMHAIN – 1st November or the first full moon after the sun enters Scorpio. It is a time when the veil between the worlds is particularly thin and a time to remember and contact those who have passed over during the year that is ending. It is also a time of new beginnings, and as such a good time to remove any negativity that has been hanging on from the previous year. It is one of the most important fire festivals and has been Christianised as All Saints Day. In recent times it is marked by the general population on November 5th as Guy Fawkes night.

YULE (WINTER SOLSTICE) – around December 21st (check ephemeris[43]). Also known as Yule. It is the time of death and rebirth of the sun as it reaches its lowest point. Christianised as Christmas (the birth of the son – i.e. sun). The Church adopted this date as representing the birth of Jesus Christ, a time adopted by previous pagan religions for the birth of their particular male (solar) deity.

IMBOLG – 1st February – or the first full moon after the sun enters Aquarius[44] (marked in the Christian calendar as Candlemass on 2nd February – a date also used by some pagans). It is a time of cleansing, renewal and preparation for growth. 'Imbolg' or 'Imbolc' appears to mean 'in the belly' [of the Goddess] or to have come from the word 'oimelc' meaning sheep's milk. The goddess Bride, Brigid or Bridget (Christianised as St Bridget) is generally worshipped on this occasion in her nurturing mothering aspects. Her totem animal is a brown cow which, where depicted, she is seen milking.

OSTARA (SPRING EQUINOX) – around 21st March (check ephemeris). Christianised as Easter although the way Easter is determined by the Church these days the two festivals can be quite far apart. It is a time when Cernnunos, Lord of the animal world, and the Green Man,

---

[43] An ephemeris is a set of tables showing the movement of all heavenly bodies throughout each and every specific year.

[44] Traditions vary and, though the full moon would seem the more accurate time to celebrate, most people seem to choose the fixed date. Personally I would prefer to celebrate at the full moon though I go along with my friends as I wish to celebrate these times with them.

Lord of the forests, are honoured and a time when the plans made during the dark winter months begin to hatch. The Babylonian pagans celebrated their new year at the spring equinox and gave eggs, painted red to symbolise life, as gifts and blessings.

BELTANE – 1st May – or the first full moon after the sun enters Taurus. Also known as May Day or Lady Day. A fertility festival and a good time for lovers. The fertility aspects are marked in some places even today with such phallic symbolism as dancing around maypoles. As with Samhain, it is a time when the veil between the Worlds is particularly thin and thus a good time for divination and spiritual contact. As part of the ritual that accompanies this festival, the High Priest, playing the part of the Oak King, is symbolically sacrificed and resurrected so that his blood is given to the land to keep it fertile.

COMHAIN (SUMMER SOLSTICE) – around 21st June (check ephemeris). The point where the Sun reaches its highest point – the height of summer and thus a natural time of balmy celebration. It has become a time when many neopagans and new ageists gather together at sacred sites such as Stonehenge and Avebury. It is a time when the Sun is honoured and traditionally this is done as the Sun rises at dawn.

LUGHNASADH – 1st August or the first full moon after the sun enters Leo. Also known as Lammas. Lugh is one of the names of the Celtic Sun Gods. It is generally seen as one of the harvest festivals, a time of feasting and fun. As part of the ritual that accompanies this festival, the High Priest, playing the part of the holly King, is symbolically sacrificed and resurrected so that his blood is given to the land to keep it fertile.

MABON (AUTUMN EQUINOX) – around 22nd September (check ephemeris). Also known as Herfest. It marks the end of the harvest time when the last sheaf of corn is cut. It is a time of gathering things together for the dark times of the Winter ahead.

As far as the solstices and equinoxes are concerned, just as the phases of the moon are followed and the varying energies are used at appropriate times for magical work (depending on the type of work at hand), so too are the phases of the sun and the wheel of the year.

Marking the wheel of the year then is more than a way of tuning in with nature and its cycles (as essential as that is) or a good excuse for a feast of celebration (though of course it is that too) but also an essential element to consider whilst working on your own personal development as well as working magic, if indeed that is what you go on to do.

PUTTING A SABBAT RITUAL TOGETHER

The Sabbat rituals, just as with the Esbat rituals, can be pieced together in building block form. As with the Esbats they begin and end with casting and closing the Circle. They would often include elements such as Drawing the Moon and Sun (bringing the Goddess and God energies into the Priestess and Priest); the Five-fold Kiss; the Charge; the blessing of cakes and wine; etc. These are generally incorporated into an extended Sabbat ritual in the middle section between casting and closing the Circle.

After each Sabbat there is a feast. The festival foods should always be of a seasonal nature as this helps emphasise the nature of the festival.

As a general rule most of the words I personally use within the Circle are in plainer modern English than that traditionally used by many Wiccan texts. I believe that in order for the mind to fully understand and react to the words being used then using 'Olde English' only serves to confuse and dilute the situation. Such language may serve to offer some sense of anti-quity to the ritual – be that genuine or otherwise – but as far as I am concerned Wicca is a path for those living in and for the here and now and therefore any antiquity, whilst respected, is unnecessary.

I have provided elements that you can include in your own rituals. As with all the ritual elements I have presented in this book, they can be pieced together in building block form, or adapted and changed to suit what feels right to you. Casting a Circle is essential if one is to work 'between the Worlds' as is the Wiccan way, as is including elements within the ritual that symbolically recognise and sympathises with the attributes of the seasonal point being marked and worked with. Outside of that remit there is plenty of scope to express one's own essential individuality as one chooses and feels fit. Take time to write the rituals out in full as you devise them yourself and keep these in your Book of Shadows. The process of writing them is an important and valuable element in itself as part of the process of tuning in to nature and its cycles and building up your own relationship to nature and those cycles.

Each ritual celebration can be adapted for use within a group (coven) situation, or for someone working on their own. If you find yourself working alone then it may be necessary to simplify the ritual. If working in a group then make the effort to include every member of that group so that everyone feels that they are taking an active role. Wicca should be designed for participants rather than for observers.

SAMHAIN

As this festival marks the end of the old year and the beginning of a new it is the time for getting rid of weaknesses and any other aspects you wish to leave behind.

With this in mind, all those taking part in the ritual should bring a small piece of parchment with them into the Circle on which has been written down weaknesses or bad habits they would like to be rid of. This is best written in red ink to represent life (some people use a dye derived from a herb known as Dragon's Blood which is wonderful if you can obtain it). It is preferable to use some form of runic script so that greater concentration will be needed for writing down the words and thus putting greater energy into the effort. After writing down the attributes that one wishes to be rid of, the parchment should be held in his or her hand and meditated upon. Samhain marks the end of the year, the equivalent of sunset in the solar cycle. It marks the end of summer and the beginning of autumn – a time of decay. We use the period between Samhain and Yule (the time of rebirth) to let all the negativity built up over the previous year to decay as appropriate to the season, in preparation for the rebirth.

This is also a time of the year when the veil between the world of the living and that of those who have passed on is particularly thin. It is therefore a time to honour those who have gone before us, especially close friends or members of our family.

SUGGESTED RITUAL

This is quite a sombre ritual and naturally so as we are clearing away weaknesses from the past year so that we can start the new year afresh, and because we are remembering the loss of loved ones from the physical plane. However, the mood can be lightened in the meditations and the more informal parts of the ritual by feeling pleased and positive about having cleared away any negativity. We can use the time when we think about those who have passed on to think or talk about the happy moments we spent with them and if we feel their presence within the Circle we can offer them our warmth. The mood can also be lightened, if it is felt appropriate, by playing some music. Food is prepared for a small feast and left within the Circle before the ritual begins.

The altar is prepared facing North with a black altar cloth. As well as the usual items on the altar there is a red candle (lit) and a black candle (lit). There is also a yellow candle (lit) upon which is a painted an image representing the sun that acknowledges the God. There is also a pomegranate and an apple. The pieces of parchment are kept by each of those who attend this ceremony. The outer edge of the Circle may be decorated with autumnal flowers, branches, pine-cones, small pump-kins, etc. There should be flowers on the altar. A cauldron or something similar to contain burning charcoal is placed in the centre of the circle (a censer will do if nothing else is available). Charcoal is put in the cauldron lit. You will also need some incense, preferably a purifying type such as lavender.

If you are lucky enough to have somewhere outside to work, which is always preferable, then a bonfire can be prepared in the centre of the circle to replace the cauldron. It is useful to take time in the weeks before Samhain to collect the wood you are going to use for the bonfire using that time to concentrate on the attributes you wish to be leave behind thus putting some of that energy into the wood to be burned and cleansed by fire.

The circle is cast and prepared in the normal way. If you choose, include the Charge of the Great Goddess and purification using the Five-fold Kiss for all participants.

Once the Goddess and God have been welcomed the Priest says: *"Now is the time of change as the wheel turns from one year to the next. As the Sun fades we move from the light into the dark and do so willingly because we know that it is simply the turning of the wheel. We look back on the past year and thank the Goddess and God for the bounty they provided for us and the lessons we have learned through the months of light."*

Priestess says: *"We stand now in a crack of time. This night belongs neither to the new year or the old and, as there is no distinction between the years, there is no distinction between the worlds. We take this opportunity to invite those we have known, loved and who have passed on from the world of form to join us in this meeting place in perfect love and perfect trust. From reuniting with our loved ones we shall all gather strength, knowing that there is no beginning or end but a continuous spiral that goes round and returns yet moves on."*

Priestess moves to stand before the yellow candle and continues . . . *"On this night we mark the end of summer and the beginning of winter. This candle represents the Lord of the Sun and by extinguishing it we mark the passing of the God of Light. Let His death show us that there are many symbolic deaths within our lives. Let us think deeply now of the things that we know must change, and the things that we must say goodbye to before the Sun once again is reborn."*

There will be a short pause here to meditate on the things that we know we must change and people and things that we wish to let go. The Priest then invites each person to light their parchments from the God candle and allowed to burn in the cauldron or thrown on to the bonfire. The Priestess and Priest burn their parchments last. When all the parchments have been burnt the incense is placed on top of the ashes to purify them. When finished, and enough time has passed for everyone to meditate on what they wish to release, the Priestess extinguishes the yellow God candle. (The candle is kept on a permanent altar or in another safe place around your home, preferably where it can be seen, until it is again lit at Yule – the Winter Solstice when the Sun is reborn).

Priest says: *"Lady and Lord, Goddess and God, out of the death of these things new seeds will be planted and from them the rebirth of new and wonderful life. So mote it be."*

All say: *"So mote it be."*

The Priest then takes the pomegranate and holds it aloft for all to see saying: *"This represents the fruit of life."*

He dramatically plunges his athame into it, thus splitting it, saying: *"Which is death!"*

He feeds some of the seeds to the Priestess first, then others in the Circle and finally takes some himself. To each he says: *"Taste the seeds of death"* before they eat the seeds.

The Priestess then picks up the apple and says: *"This represents the fruit of death."*

The Priestess then cuts the apple crosswise saying: *"Which is life!"*

She hold the apple up to show the pentacle formed by the seeds and says: *"The apple is a fruit of healing and contains the five fold star of rebirth."*

A bite of the apple is taken by all, the Priest first and finally the Priestess. To each the Priestess says: *"Taste the seeds of rebirth"* before they take a bite.

The Priestess (as the representative of the Goddess) then faces and addresses the Priest (as the representative of the God) saying: *"Through you all passes from life, but through Me all may be reborn. Everything passes, everything changes. Seed becomes fruit; fruit becomes seed. Love me and trust me without fear in your heart. My womb is the cauldron of rebirth, through me the circle is ever turning. So mote it be."*

All say: *"So mote it be."*

Priest and Priestess salute each other with a kiss.

Priest then bows to the Priestess and says: *"Goddess of love, magic and wisdom, whisper in our ears whatever you may, and trust that the knowledge you share with us is used wisely. Allow us to use your powers to bring potency to our spells and rituals, for the good of all, according to the free will of all. So mote it be."*

All say: *"So mote it be."*

Time is then taken to enjoy the feast. Those within the circle can laugh and joke, dance or just chat if they please. The Priestess shall be responsible for judging when enough time has passed to end the ceremony.

Priest says: *"We came together in love and friendship; let us part the same way. Let us spread the love we have known in this Circle outward to all."*

Athames are raised in salute.

Priestess says: *"Lady and Lord, Goddess and God, our thanks to you for sharing this time with us. Our thanks for watching over us; guarding and guiding us in all things. Love is the Law and Love is the Bond. Merry did we meet, merry do we part, merry may we meet again."*

The Circle is closed in the normal way.

YULE (WINTER SOLSTICE)

It is no coincidence that the Christian Christmas coincides with Yule. To a Christian, Christmas marks the birth of the Son of God. It is derived from much older pagan traditions (as is common throughout Christianity, though few recognise it) which mark the birth (or rebirth) of the Sun God. Pagan elements are rife throughout the traditional Christian Christmas celebrations. The evergreen tree signifies the continuance of life; the silver and gold sparkly baubles help to encourage the new light into the home (and could equally represent the Goddess and Gold). Holly with its red berries can be seen to represent the final death of the Holly King. Mistletoe with its white berries (which if squeezed one will notice are extraordinarily semen like) represents fertility (hence the tradition of kissing underneath a mistletoe sprig).

SUGGESTED RITUAL

The ceremony should normally be held as close as possible to the actual moment of the solstice. The altar is prepared in the normal way, facing East. Outside of where the Circle is to be cast, behind the Eastern candle there should be a traditional Yule fir tree, or something else representing the season. Plenty of candles should be placed around the ceremonial area to bring light. Incense to be used on the altar could be something seasonal such as a mixture of frankincense and myrrh. Also on the altar should be the yellow God candle that was extinguished at Samhain. Some seasonal food and wine should also be available within the Circle area.

The Priestess wears red robes, Priest wears black robes over the top of his white robes. There is a single white candle burning in the centre of the room with other white candles (unlit) at the four quarters. If working alone, then starting with black robes and changing to white later would be appropriate unless you choose to work skyclad of course.

Yule is the time when the Holly King, God of the waning year, gives way to the Oak King, God of the waxing year. The sun has reached its lowest point and starts to rise again. The Sun is reborn. It is traditional to include a large Yule log of oak to be burnt if you are lucky enough to have an open fire. Saving the ashes from the previous year's celebrations to be added to the current year's log helps to signify the continuance of the cycle.

The circle is cast and prepared in the normal way. Drawing down the Sun by the Priestess into the Priest would be particularly appropriate to include for this ritual.

The Priest sits in front of the unlit yellow (God) candle staring into it. This is the candle extinguished and saved from Samhain.

The Priestess casts the Circle in the normal way (lighting the four white candles on the way).

Others stand in a circle around the Priest, the Priestess stands in the West with the others in the circle.

The others start moving slowly deosil, the Priestess moves slowly widdershins weaving in and out of the others. As she passes the candles at the quarters she snuffs them out. Whilst doing this she says:

As the wheel turns, the days have grown shorter,
The trees and flowers have gone into slumber.

The darkness of the winter has taken hold,
As the Holly King himself has become old and decayed.

After the last quarter candle has been snuffed out and the Priestess has been around the circle back to the West, the circle stops moving. All but the Priestess turn their backs to face outwards. The Priestess moves forward and snuffs out the remaining white candle on the altar leaving the place in darkness. The Priest removes his black robes to reveal white robes underneath.

The Priestess says:

Now, in the depths of winter,
The waning of the year is accomplished.
The reign of the Holly King is over,
And he has left us to rest in the underworld.

But the wheel still turns as the seasons change,
And the Oak King must return to rule with glory.

Priestess kisses Priest and lights central white candle and the yellow candle.

Behold, the Sun is reborn.
He is the child of promise from the Great Mother's womb.
He is the Lord, our Sun, who is born again.
Set aside all darkness and tears,
And look instead to the coming year.

Priestess moves to the East and joins the circle. The circle starts to rotate again, deosil, with the Priestess moving with them lighting the quarter candles as she passes. Priest stands up and adopts God position with head raised.

▲ *God position.*

All does change,
As the new replaces the old,
And the wheel of the season goes on,
Ever the same, ever changing.

Goddess and God, grant us your favours,
Of joy, of love, of peace,
And give them to the world,
That needs your blessings so deeply.

Blessed Be."

The cakes and wine are blessed.

The Circle is closed in the normal way. This can be followed by plenty of feasting and drinking, the giving of presents and general festivities.

IMBOLG

Imbolg (or Imbolc, pronounced 'immolg') marks the first stirrings of the year. The emphasis is on light rather than heat, the first sign that Spring is on the way. It is Christianised as Candlemass and does indeed traditionally involve a great many candles to help invite the light into your life and your home. Brigid, as the Mother Goddess and bringer of fire, is worshipped at this time, the ritual marks the fertilising of the seed in her belly. Between Samhain and Yule we spent time getting rid of any negative energies from the previous year and started making plans for the coming year. We use Imbolg as a time to 'fertilise the seed' and start putting in place those things we need to make those plans that we made become a reality.

This particular ritual requires the High Priestess to pick two other women together to represent the triple Goddess in the aspects of Maiden, Mother and Crone. The Maiden will require a small bouquet of fresh flowers: spring flowers are preferable. The Crone will need a dark scarf to wear over her head or a cloak with a hood. A crown of small candles is traditionally made for the High Priestess to wear. Careful use of some tin foil is essential if the High Priestess is not to set fire to her hair. The High Priest wears black robes. If working alone, white, red and black candles can be used to represent the Maiden, Mother and Crone aspects of the Goddess.

The altar is dressed up in spring time flowers such as snow drops and daffodils, the altar cloth being a bright yellow and in the North of the Circle. Plenty of candles are lit in the room to keep the whole ceremony as bright as possible. Candles are lit in each window to encourage the light into your home and traditionally the door is left ajar for as long as possible.

A straw effigy or corn dolly is made to represent Brigid's child. This is known as a 'Biddy'. A phallic shaped wand is also required. Three evergreen twigs are placed on the altar. An extra pair of candles is required – either one black and one white; or one red and one green (representing the two polarities of masculine and feminine.) A broom is placed by the altar and a cauldron in the centre of the Circle.

The Circle is cast in the normal way. Everyone within the Circle begins to dance around the altar in couples or solo. When the High Priestess is satisfied that this has raised the energy within the Circle the High Priest stands with his back to the altar and the High Priestess stands in front of him to invoke the Dark Lord into him. She gives him the five-fold kiss, and he does the same to her.

High Priestess says:

"Dark Lord of the Shadows,
Lord of Death and Resurrection,
You who takes life and gives it anew,
Encourage our hearts,

And let your light crystallise in our blood,
Fulfilling the resurrection,
Descend, we pray you,
Upon this your servant and High Priest."

Everyone visualises the Lord of the Underworld manifesting in the High Priest. The High Priest draws an invoking pentagram of Earth in the air in front of the High Priestess and says: *"Blessed Be."*

The High Priest moves to one side and watches while the Maiden, Mother and Crone prepare 'Brigid's bed'. They lay the Biddy and the phallic wand side by side in the centre of the circle, besides the cauldron, with their heads facing towards the altar. The Maiden takes the white candle from the alter and places it to the right of the Biddy, the Crone takes the black candle and places it to the left. The mother takes a light from the altar candle and lights them both. The Maiden, Mother and Crone then stand in front of the Altar facing South between the altar and the Biddy – the Maiden to the right of the Mother and the Crone to her left. The High Priest moves to the South and faces them. He takes the crown of candles, lights the candles and places the crown on the head of the Mother Goddess. He then takes the bouquet of flowers and places them in the hands of the Maiden. He takes the dark scarf and places it over the head of the Crone – or raises her hood if she is wearing a cloak.

The High Priest then stands back and declares:

"Behold the Goddess in her three aspects,
Maiden, Mother and Crone.
Who is as ever one within us all.
Without Spring there can be no Summer,
Without Summer no Winter,
And without Winter no Spring."

"I call upon you, Mighty Mother of us all, bringer of all fruitfulness, by seed and root, by bud and stem, by leaf and flower and fruit, by love do I invoke you to descend upon the body of this your servant and priestess."

The High Priest then Draws down the Moon into the High Priestess as others visualise the Great Goddess manifesting in her.

She then recites the Charge of the Great Goddess . . .

"Listen to the words of the Great Goddess,
who throughout time has been known by many names.
Assemble in a sacred place of your own making when the Moon is full,
and any other time you have need of My aid.
Know that My love will make you free,
for nobody can prevent your worship of Me in your mind and your heart.
Listen well when you worship,

and I will teach you the deep mysteries, ancient and powerful.
I require no sacrifices or pain, for I am the Mother of all things,
the Creatress who made you out of My love,
and the One who endures through all time.
"I am the beauty of the Earth, the green of growing things.
I am the white Moon whose light is full among the stars and soft upon the Earth.
From Me all things are born, to Me all things, in their seasons return.
Let My worship be in your hearts, for all acts of love and pleasure are My rituals.
You see Me in the love of man and woman,
the love of parent and child, the love of humans to all My creations.
When you create with your hands, I am there.
I blow the breath of life into the seeds you plant, whether of plant or child.
I stand beside you always, whispering soft words of wisdom and guidance.
You need only to listen."

The Maiden then takes the broom from beside the altar and ritually sweeps around the Circle (deosil) to sweep out the old ready for the new, she then returns to the others in front of the altar. The High Priest kneels before the Maiden, Mother and Crone in front of the cauldron. He takes the three evergreen twigs and lights them from the candles placed either side of the Biddy and lets them burn for a while in the cauldron. He takes the Biddy and passes her three times through the smoke.

High Priest:

"We have banished Winter,
and welcome Spring,
Say farewell to what is dead,
And welcome new life in."

The High Priest blows out the candles from the Mother's crown and removes it, placing it back on the altar as he does with the Maiden's flowers and the Crone's scarf. The Maiden, Mother and Crone place the Biddy on the altar with the phallic wand and the candles.

The Great Rite is performed.

The cakes and wine are blessed by the High Priestess and High Priest.

The Circle is then closed in the normal way and followed by a feast as usual.

OSTARA (SPRING EQUINOX)

Ostara equates with the Christian festival of Easter, though ironically Easter is determined by the moon's cycle and is thus often quite late. It is the celebration of spring – the resurrection of the fertility of the land – the power of the sun is gradually getting stronger. It is a wonderfully joyous time with many trees coming back to life and shoots beginning to emerge through the ground, and this should be reflected in the celebration. It is a time of the year where the plans and aspirations that we had back at Yule and Imbolg start to be implemented. Just as the new shoots start coming through the ground, so too should that which we wish to manifest in our life show the first signs of coming to be.

Being an equinox it is also a time of great balance when the length of the day is equal to the length of the night. Spend some time in your meditations tuning into this sense of balance.

SUGGESTED RITUAL

A wheel symbol needs to be made and decorated with seasonal flowers as a centrepiece for the altar. This represents the ever-turning wheel of the year. This can be made out of anything you feel is suitable, though using some thin fronds from a weeping willow tree as a base is pretty good for the occasion.

This ritual is best held outside so that a proper fire may be built within the cauldron. If it is necessary to hold the celebration indoors, for the purposes of privacy or because of the weather, then the cauldron is placed in the centre of the Circle and instead of a full fire it is loaded with a number of candles – I would suggest up to five. The altar is in the North. The wheel symbol is placed on the altar which is decorated with yet more seasonal flowers.

The Circle is cast in the normal way. The High Priestess stands in the East, the High Priest in the West, and others stand around the circumference of the Circle with man and woman alternating as far as possible.

High Priestess steps forwards, lights a taper from the altar and sets light to the cauldron (or lights the candles) saying:

"We kindle this fire today, in the presence of the Lady and Lord, Goddess and God, without malice, jealousy, envy or fear of anything under the Sun."

"Light of Life, be a bright flame before us, be a guiding star above us and a smooth path beneath our feet. Kindle the flame in our hearts, a flame for our neighbours, our foes, friends and kindred all."

The High Priestess moves around the Circle to stand in front of the High Priest and draws an invoking Fire pentagram in front of him using the wand, gives him a kiss then hands the wand to him. He uses the wand to do the same to her they then lead the others deosil around the Circle and leap the fire. They continue to do this until the fire begins to die down. When all is finished each should receive the five-fold kiss from the opposite gender to purify them.

The cakes and wine are blessed by the High Priestess and High Priest.

The Circle is closed in the normal way and feasting, drinking and chat follows.

BELTANE

Beltane is the time of year when everything is beginning to come into full bloom. Blossom adorns the trees, flowers start flourishing everywhere, it is a time when fertility is at its height and this is reflected in the celebrations. Pagan style celebrations from the past have survived to the present day with obvious fertility elements such as dancing around the maypole (a phallic symbol if ever there was one) and crowning a young maiden as the May Queen.

Beltane is a time for lovers. It is a wonderful time to rekindle your relationship with your loved one and if you are lucky enough to have a partner who shares your ways it is a good time for a little light hearted frolicking and offering lovers' gifts to each other. A man may even wish to make a crown out of willow fronds, decorated with hawthorn blossoms, with which to crown his May Queen.

It is a time when those plans that started to grow at Ostara should be coming into flower and growing nicely. Use the energy of Beltane to add weight to those plans to help them come to full fruition.

SUGGESTED RITUAL

This ritual is in two parts. The second part includes the analogous ritual sacrifice of the Oak King acted out by the High Priestess and High Priest. This is performed so that the 'blood' of the sacrificed King ensures the continued fertility of the land (and one's own plans) and he is resurrected through the power of the Goddess so that he can continue his reign through to the height of summer. If working alone this will obviously prove problematic, but visualising the ritual may prove to be a reasonable substitute.

The altar is placed in the north of the Circle to allow plenty of room. On the altar you will need the pentacle; the North candle behind the Pentacle, two altar candles (preferably silver and gold), chalice of wine, water, salt, athames, censer, nuts, hawthorn, blackthorn. And a see-through green scarf.

A cauldron is placed in the South with a white candle burning in it. Tapers are ready beside the cauldron. One for each person in the Circle. If outdoors, the 'old Bel-fire' should be a protected candle, but the 'new Bel-fire' should be a real (small) bonfire. The High Priest remains outside of the Circle with the other participants, standing at the North-East edge, while the High Priestess casts it in the normal way.

High Priestess admits the High Priest into the Circle with a kiss, moving deosil. The High Priest turns to welcome the next participant in the same way who in turn welcomes the next, preferably with opposite genders in turn. Once all have entered the Circle, the High Priestess picks up her athame and closes the gateway, with three sweeps whilst visualising the Circle being re-sealed.

High Priestess stands with her back to the altar – athame in right hand – in Goddess position.

▲ *Goddess position.*

High Priest kneels before her and bows with arms spread wide in reverence. He then gives her the Five-fold Kiss.

High Priest stands before the High Priestess in God position with head bowed and says: "*I call upon you, Mighty Mother of us all, bringer of all fruitfulness, by seed and root, by bud and stem, by leaf and flower and fruit, by love do I invoke you to descend upon the body of this your servant and priestess*".

During this he touches her lightly on the right breast, left breast and womb and finally the right breast again. He then returns to a kneeling position and spreads his arms outwards and downwards with the palms forward saying:

149

"Hail Mighty Mother Goddess!
Pour forth your store of love.
I bow before you, and adore you to the end.
With loving sacrifice I shall adorn your shrine.
Your foot is my lip..."

He kisses right foot and says

"...my prayer upbourne
Upon the rising incense-smoke; then spend
Your ancient love, O Mighty One, descend
To aid me who without you am forlorn."

High Priest stands and takes a backward step but remains facing the High Priestess.

High Priestess draws an invoking pentagram of Earth in front of High Priest saying:

"Of the Mother darksome and Divine,
Mine the scourge, and mine the kiss,
The five point star of love and bliss,
Here I charge you in this sign."

She then recites the Charge of the Great Goddess...

"Listen to the words of the Great Goddess,
who throughout time has been known by many names.
Assemble in a sacred place of your own making when the Moon is full,
and any other time you have need of My aid.
Know that My love will make you free,
for nobody can prevent your worship of Me in your mind and your heart.
Listen well when you worship,
and I will teach you the deep mysteries, ancient and powerful.
I require no sacrifices or pain, for I am the Mother of all things,
the Creatress who made you out of My love,
and the One who endures through all time.

"I am the beauty of the Earth, the green of growing things.
I am the white Moon whose light is full among the stars and soft upon the Earth.
From Me all things are born, to Me all things, in their seasons return.
Let My worship be in your hearts, for all acts of love and pleasure are My rituals.
You see Me in the love of man and woman,
the love of parent and child, the love of humans to all My creations.
When you create with your hands, I am there.
I blow the breath of life into the seeds you plant, whether of plant of child.
I stand beside you always, whispering soft words of wisdom and guidance.
You need only to listen."

The Great Rite is then performed (see page 128)

The cauldron is moved to the centre of the circle. The following part of the ceremony is the ritual enactment of the death of the Oak King.

The High Priest picks up the scarf, gathers it lengthways like a rope and holds it one end in each hand. He makes towards the High Priestess (who starts to clap rhythmically along with all the other participants) as if to throw the scarf over her shoulders. She eludes him tantalisingly. The High Priestess weaves in and out of the coven members while the High Priest tries to 'capture' her.

After a while the High Priestess allows the High Priest to catch her. They kiss and separate. Once again the High Priest pursues the High Priestess, only this time more solemnly and slowly. (He is dying.) The High Priestess is more solemn as she leads him to his death. The pursuit continues till the High Priestess puts herself between the cauldron and the altar, facing the altar. The High Priest stops with his back to the altar and captures her with his scarf. They embrace wholeheartedly and after a few seconds the High Priest allows the scarf to fall from his hands. The High Priestess releases him and takes a step backwards.

The High Priest drops to his knees and sits back on his heels, lowering his head, chin on chest.

The High Priestess spreads her arms. High Priestess picks up the scarf and holds it over the High Priest and slowly releases it like a shroud.

The High Priestess extinguishes the altar candles, but keeps the Earth candle burning.

High Priestess returns to stand before the High Priest.

The High Priest turns and kneels, close to and facing the cauldron. The High Priest stays kneeling but 'dead'.

When everyone is in place, The High Priestess blows out the candle in the cauldron and is silent for a moment.

Then says: *"The Bel Fire is extinguished and the Oak king is dead. He has embraced the great Mother and died of his love. So it has been, year by year since time began. Yet if the Oak King is dead, he who is God of the Waxing year – all is dead. The fields bear no crops, the trees bear no fruit, and the creatures of the Great Mother bear no young. What shall we do therefore, that the Oak King may live again?"*

All (except High Priest) say: *"Rekindle the Bel-fire! So it must be."*

The High Priestess takes a taper, rises, goes to the altar, lights the taper from the Earth candle and kneels again at the cauldron relighting the candle within. The High Priestess then lights a second taper for herself. She rises to face the High Priest and raises the scarf laying it on the floor.

The High Priestess then relights the altar candles and if outside lights the bonfire.

The High Priestess holds out one of the tapers to the High Priest and says: *"Come back to us Oak King, so that the land may once again be fruitful."*
The High Priest rises, accepts the taper and says:

"I am a stag of 7 tines,
I am a flood on a plain,
I am a wind on the deep waters,
I am a shining tear of the sun,
I am a hawk on a cliff,
I am fair among flowers,
I am a god who sets the head afire with smoke."

The High Priest and High Priestess now link hands and join hands with all the other participants who begin to skip around the cauldron in a deosil direction.
They chant:

"Oh do not tell the priest of our plight,
Or he would call it a sin!
But we shall be out in the woods all night,
A conjuring Summer in!
And we bring you news by word of mouth,
Good news for cattle and corn,
Now the sun is come up from the South,
With Oak and Ash and Thorn."

They repeat "Oak Ash and Thorn" ad lib. The circle should gradually move faster and faster. Every now and then in pairs they break away and jump the cauldron or the bonfire. When the energy has been raised, the High Priest cries: *"Down!"*
All sit down, thoroughly ground themselves and enjoy laughing and joking or whatever occurs.
When ready the High Priest kneels in front of High Priestess holding up the plate of cakes and nuts. The High Priestess draws an invoking Earth pentagram over the nuts.
High Priest says: *"O queen most secret, bless this food into our bodies, bestowing health, wealth, strength, joy and peace and that fulfilment of love which is perfect happiness."*
High Priestess places athame on altar, kisses High Priest, takes a nut. She kisses him again and he takes a nut. Others in the Circle are each handed the plate of nuts, man to woman, woman to man, each taking a nut.
The Circle is then closed in the normal way.

▲ *Sancreed Well, Cornwall, has strong healing energies.*

▲ *Merry Maidens Circle, Cornwall, used as a meeting place today by many including druids.*

▲ *Tregeseal Circle, near St Just, Cornwall, a circle that I use for special occasions.*

▲ *Ballowall Barrow on the cliffs above Cape Cornwall, used as a burial chamber and for ritual magic going back to the bronze age.*

This is a good night to get out into the countryside, if you are lucky enough to be close to countryside, or a local park if you live in the City. Getting out to one of the sacred sites, such as Avebury, Glastonbury Tor, and joining the festivities with other pagans throughout the night is a wonderfully uplifting and empowering experience.

COMHAIN (MIDSUMMER SOLSTICE)

At Beltane the Oak King was ritually sacrificed and resurrected. At midsummer, when the Sun is at its strongest and highest, the Oak King, who rules the waxing half of the year, hands over his reign to the Holly King who rules the waning half of the year. Just as the different phases of the Lunar month are represented by different aspects of the Goddess, so too are different phases of the Solar year represented by different aspects of the God.

Rise early to greet the sunrise. If you can make it to a sacred site to join others then all the better. Modern day Druids tend to gather at Stonehenge as this is one of their biggest Sabbats (being more solar oriented). Comhain is a time to fully enjoy the strength of the sun and the joys of summer. Open your heart to the sun's energies and charge yourself up.

SUGGESTED RITUAL

This ritual is best suited for out of doors, though it can be enacted indoors if necessary. Out of doors two small bonfires are built inside the Circle, one slightly to the North of the other. If indoors these will need to replaced with candles. The cauldron is placed in front of the altar, which is in the North, full of summer flowers. Two crowns are made, one of oak leaves and the other of holly leaves. A number of differing length straws are placed on the altar, a number equal to the number of men in the Circle, barring the High Priest. (For this ritual you will thus require at least three men including the High Priest.) There is a black silk or cotton scarf on the altar as well as a sprig of heather.

The Circle is prepared and opened as normal. The men are to draw lots to see who will be sacrificed as the Oak King and who will take over as a representative of the Holly King. The High Priestess declares: *"Let the men draw lots."*

The Maiden takes the straws from the altar and hiding their length allows each man to draw a straw. The High Priestess points to the man who has drawn the longest straw and declares: *"You are the Oak King, Maiden bring his crown."*

The maiden places the oak crown on top of the chosen man's head. The High Priestess points to the man who has drawn the shortest straw and declares: *"You are the Holly King, Maiden bring his crown."*

The Maiden places the holly crown on top of the chosen man's head. The High Priestess leads the Oak King to stand in the centre of the Circle facing West and then joins the High Priest in front of the altar. The Holly King moves to stand in front of the Oak King, places his hands on his shoulders and wrestles him to the ground. When the Oak King falls to his knees (as he must) the Maiden ties the blindfold around his eyes. The High Priestess takes up her athame and begins to dance deosil around the Oak King as the High Priest reads the following poem in a rhythmic fashion:

Dance, dance, dance Lady, round and around,
Dance your dance on the Oak King's crown.

Dance, dance, dance on the Oak Kings' tomb,
Dance Lady, dance as he enters your womb.

Dance, dance, dance at the Holly Kings' birth,
Who has killed his brother for the love of the Earth.

Dance, Lady dance to the Sun God's power,
With his touch of gold on every field and flower.

Dance, dance, dance with your blade in hand,
To summon the Sun, and to bless the land.

Dance, Lady dance for the Holly Kings' reign,
Dance, dance, dance till Oak rises again.

Dance, Lady dance . . . Dance, Lady dance . . . (the rest of the coven join in as the rhythm gets faster and faster. The High Priestess ends her dance when the High Priest signals to everyone else to stop the chant and she then lays her athame down on the altar. The Maiden and the High Priestess help the Oak King to rise and kneel back down in front of the Western Candle.

High Priestess says: *"The spirit of the Oak King has passed from us to rest until the turning of the wheel announces his return to rule at Yule."*

The Maiden takes the blindfold off of the Oak King who leaves his crown in the West and rejoins the coven.

High Priest says: *"Let the Midsummer fires be lit."*

The Holly King and the Maiden light a taper from the altar candle and each light one of the two bonfires (or candles). The Maiden takes the High Priest's athame and stands in the West facing in. The Holly King takes the Chalice and stands in the East facing in. The High Priest and the High Priestess symbolically enact the Great Rite with the Maiden and the Holly King passing them their Chalice and blade at the appropriate moment. High Priest stands and moves in front of the cauldron, taking the wand from the altar and putting down his athame.

High Priestess invokes: *"Great power of the heavens, bring back your light to protect this land. Lift your shining spear high, and drive out the darkness so that we may stand on the hill of vision with the green path leading us to the realm of the Gods".*

She draws an invoking pentagram of Earth with her fingers in front of the High Priest who lifts the wand above his head and plunges it into the cauldron saying: *"The spear to the cauldron, Lance to the Grail, Spirit into flesh, without fail."*

The High Priestess stands and takes the heather, dips it into the cauldron whilst the High Priest leads the coven deosil around the Circle. As they all pass through between the two bonfires she consecrates them and follows the last person through herself.

The Circle is closed in the normal way. A feast of summer fruits is then eaten.

LUGHNASADH

At Beltane, the Oak King is symbolically sacrificed and resurrected in order that his blood is given to the land in order to maintain its fertility. At Lughnasadh it is the turn of the Holly King to be symbolically sacrificed and resurrected for the same reason.

Lughnasadh marks the start of the harvest season. The corn in the fields is ripe and the fruits on the trees are getting to the point where they are ready to be picked. It is the time when we start to reap the rewards of the work we have put in through the year. Look at the positive things that have happened and give thanks for them and hold them close knowing that we have done the best we can.

SUGGESTED RITUAL

The altar is placed in the North. On it is a small loaf and a green scarf. The High Priest wears a crown of holly leaves to represent the Holly King.

The Circle is cast in the normal way.

The High Priest picks up the scarf, gathers it lengthways like a rope and holds one end in each hand. He makes towards the High Priestess (who starts to clap rhythmically) as if to throw the scarf over her shoulders. She eludes him tantalisingly. (Here she would weave in and out of the coven members whilst the High Priest tries to 'capture' her.)

After a while the High Priestess allows the High Priest to catch her. They kiss and separate. Once again the High Priest pursues the High

Priestess Only this time more solemnly and slowly. (He is 'dying'). The High Priestess is more solemn as she leads him to his death. The pursuit continues till the High Priestess puts herself between the cauldron and the altar, facing the altar. The High Priest stops with his back to the altar and captures her with his scarf. They embrace wholeheartedly and after a few seconds the High Priest allows the scarf to fall from his hands. The High Priestess releases him and takes a step backwards.

The High Priest drops to his knees and sits back on his heels, lowering his head, chin on chest.

The High Priestess calls for two other women to step forward. The three of them (representing the triple Goddess aspects of Maiden, Mother and Crone) tower over the High Priest and each get hold of the scarf. They release the scarf over the head of the High Priest like a shroud.

The High Priestess then turns to the altar and takes the small loaf which she holds over the bowed head of the High Priest, then turns to hold it high above the altar and says: *"Mighty Mother, Goddess of fruitfulness, bless this bread with your body."*

She turns to the High Priest again and says to all: *"Gather around, children of the harvest."*

Everyone within the Circle moves in close to surround the kneeling High Priest. The High Priestess then says: *"The Holly King is dead. He embraced the Mighty Mother and died of his love. But if the Holly King is dead – our Lord of the Waning Year – then all is dead and all that sleeps in the womb of the Earth would sleep for all time. What shall we do so that the Holly King may live again?"*

The Maiden replies: *"Give him the bread of life so that his sleep will lead on to rebirth."*

The High Priestess says*: "So it must be."*

She breaks the bread into small pieces, keeping a little to leave as an offering to the Earth at the end of the ceremony, and gives a piece to each person in the Circle. She does not take a piece for herself yet. The Maiden and Crone lift the scarf from the High Priest's head and let it drop to the floor. The High Priestess offers him a piece of bread saying: *"Come back to us, Holly King, so that the land can be fruitful once more."*

The High Priestess eats a piece of bread with the High Priest. The High Priest rises and says:

"I am a battle-waging spear;[45]
I am a salmon in the pool;

---

[45] These lines relate to the months of the Celtic tree calendar covering the half of the year ruled by the Holly King. The verse used at Beltane (I am a stag of seven tines) is the half ruled by the Oak King.

I am a hill of poetry;
I am a ruthless boar;
I am a threatening noise of the winter's sea;
I am a wave of the sea;
Who but I can unfold the secrets of the unhewn dolmen?"[46]

The High Priestess then leads the Circle in a dance in a deosil direction gradually getting faster and faster until she shouts: *"Down!"* at which point everyone sits.

The Great Rite is enacted. The Circle is closed in the normal way and the feast is eaten.

MABON

The two Equinoxes are times of equilibrium. Day and night are matched (Equinox literally means 'equal night') and the tide of the year flows steadily. The Autumn Equinox's theme is that of rest after labour – of repose. The Sun is about to enter the sign of Libra – the Balance.

Times of balance are, by their nature, times when the veil between the seen and unseen is thin. It is, therefore, a time when we can expect an increase in spectral appearances from beyond the veil. In the Celtic tree calendar the Autumn Equinox falls in between the Vine month and Ivy – both of which grow spirally. The spiral (the double spiral in particular) is a symbol of reincarnation. The bird of the Autumn Equinox is the Swan —a symbol of the immortality of the soul.

The Autumn Equinox marks the completion of the harvest, and thanksgiving for abundance, with the emphasis on the future return of that abundance. It is a time when we complete the process of giving thanks for what the year has provided and gathering things together for the darkest months ahead.

SUGGESTED RITUAL

The altar is placed in the North and is decorated with pine cones, oak sprigs, acorns and ears of corn.

The Circle is cast in the normal way.

The High Priest stands in the West in the God position and head raised with his athame and the High Priestess in the East in the Goddess position with the phallic wand. Others stand around the circumference of the Circle with man and woman alternating as far as possible.

---

[46] A dolmen is a burial chamber – a 'womb of the Earth' in which a body is buried in a position like that of a foetus in the womb.

The High Priestess says:

"Now is the time of balance,
when Day and Night face each other as equals.
Yet at this season the Night is waxing and the Day is waning;
for nothing remains without change,
in the tides of the Earth and Sky.
Know and remember,
that whatsoever rises must also set,
and whatsoever sets must also rise.
Farewell Sun, ever returning light,
The hidden God, whoever yet remains,
Depart to the Land Of Youth,
Through the gates of death,
to dwell enthroned until you return again.
Even as you diminish in strength,
Lord you continue to live within ourselves,
As does the seed of flesh,
Hidden in the Earth."

The High Priestess moves deosil around the Circle to stand before the High Priest and gives him a kiss. He places his athame to one side and kisses her, she hands him the wand and they lead the others in a procession around the Circle.

Spend some time meditating on the months that lay ahead.

Cakes and wine are blessed.

Close the Circle in the normal way.

18

INITIATION AND RITES OF PASSAGE

Everyone goes through a series of initiations in life. They mark our transit from one stage of development to the next. The first initiation we all experience is birth, inevitably a traumatic experience even if we retain little memory of the process in our every day consciousness. We then have other initiations such as puberty, the acceptance into adulthood (generally in a Christian dominated society at 18 or 21), for some there is marriage or hand-fasting, entering middle age, old age, and death.

Unfortunately in this age, some of these transitions are not properly marked. I feel it would make a great difference and avoid many problems if they were marked formally. For instance, there is a period in the life of a young boy or girl (around the age of 7) where they feel that it is time that they are treated less as a child and more as a young man or woman. If this is not acknowledged by the parents then it can start to lead into a bit of a battleground with the young person trying desperately to be treated differently but without the maturity or confidence to sit down and express what they are feeling and what they need. A simple ceremony involving the young person and parents, siblings, and possibly other relations, could easily avoid such situations and the months of trauma that goes with it on both sides, by openly marking this transit in the young person's life. There are other transits, that also often go unmarked and yet would benefit from such a ceremony (as they have in times past) such as puberty in the early teens (around the age of 14 . . . note the 7 year period).

These transits, or periods of initiation (whether marked formally or not) can be seen as 'outer' initiations. There are also 'inner' initiations that we reach generally later in life. They are the periods in our life when we suddenly recognise and have to come to terms with the inner self and our spiritual aspects. For a potential Wiccan then one shall reach a period when one accepts an essential pagan orientation to their world view and a spirituality that is closely aligned to nature. As it is opening up oneself to a deeply personal understanding of one's inner self it is good to mark such an occasion alone so that it can remain entirely personal without any pressure whatsoever from outside influences. A self-dedication ceremony written and devised by oneself would be ideal. An example has been provided below to provide ideas for a general framework, but adapting this to suit one's own view is not only highly recommended but essential.

In Wicca there are two other forms of initiation. There are the three degree initiations that mark one's development and progress through the teachings under the guidance of a High Priestess and/or High Priest. There is also, generally, an initiatory process that one may go through when joining a new group or coven that is designed to introduce the newcomer to the group mind set. For a witch who chooses to work as a solitary there is, by definition, not a great opportunity of entering into the initiation process and all the many and varied benefits that can be gained from working with this process in association with others.

It is possible to dedicate oneself to the Goddess and God and carry this through to initiate oneself to the first degree using a similar ceremony. It should be borne in mind, however, that whilst some covens accept the idea of self initiation, this is not universally accepted within Wicca. To progress beyond the first stage it is necessary to find a trusted adept who you feel totally comfortable working with as it is important to have someone who is able to be objective to help guide you. It needs to be someone who has already been through the process and thus in a position to appreciate what you are going through and what you need to learn. This would most likely be the High Priestess or High Priest from your own coven, if that is how you work, or someone with whom you associate on a less formal basis, but with whom you communicate regularly and who has followed and guided your personal development closely enough to ascertain whether or not you have reached a level that demands initiation to further your progress. Both you and the High Priestess/High Priest need to feel certain that you are ready for any initiation. If the High Priestess/High Priest feels that you are not ready, then if they are any good they will tell you what they feel you need to do in order to prepare yourself in as kind a way as possible. If they are worthy of the title they hold then the reasons they give shall ring true and you shall understand that more work is needed, and be given a reasonable idea of the sort of work you need to undertake.

There are three degrees of initiation.

The first degree is when one is introduced and welcomed to the Circle. A first degree witch is neither bound to the Craft, nor free to turn away easily, yet there is still that option. A first degree witch becomes a Priestess or Priest of the Craft but is still very much a beginner. They are made a Priestess or Priest as in Wicca it is the objective to experience the divine personally and directly. The first degree ceremony should enable this relationship to open up if it hasn't already done so. The first degree Wiccan is formally introduced to the working tools and welcomed into inner Circle of those initiating them.

A second degree initiation is very similar to the first degree. A second degree witch will have become adept at using all the tools of the Craft, will be well versed and practised at casting the Circle and developed many personal skills including the ability to hold and work the energies of a Circle. The second degree initiation thoroughly binds the witch to the service of the Goddess and God for life – not something to be undertaken lightly – and will have a reasonable idea regarding the form of service that their dedication is likely to take. A second degree witch is almost certainly going to be of a standard where they are able to start teaching and guiding others on the path. At the second degree one shall have learnt to work confidently with the elements, even though the spirit may not yet have fully progressed to the point where it stands firmly above the elements having fully mastered them. In some traditions a second degree Wiccan is given the title of High Priestess or High Priest. This can open up all sorts of egotistical glamours that can indeed prove to be a great test, providing one with a challenge that needs to be overcome, but one that I personally find unnecessarily painful. The challenge of the ego can be dealt with in a far gentler way with the continued guidance of a good third degree High Priestess or Priest. A second degree Wiccan should be able to conduct a first degree initiation and to undertake more responsibilities within the group such as helping to write rituals, devise spells for specific work, and help train those working towards the first degree and beyond.

A third degree witch is one who has taken one step further, one who is then a High Priestess or High Priest and who has taken the vow to live as one with the Goddess and God and who has symbolically joined as one with them. A third degree witch will have developed to the point where they are able to run their own Coven, be in a position to act as a teacher and guide to those who seek knowledge and who have dedicated them-selves to the Craft and the will of the Goddess and God. They will discover that the third degree is but the third of seven stages of develop-ment, the seventh not being reached on the physical plane within the world of the living. No further initiations are necessary. The third degree witch will be well aware when they have transcended a further barrier of development and will recognise the breadth of knowledge that is available to him or her which they have a responsibility to accumu-late, assimilate and distribute as best they can.

One of the aims of the process of initiation is to fully open the energy flows throughout the body's chakras that were discussed earlier in this book. When we are born the chakras are bound by a protective web of etheric substance that inhibits the flow of natural energies through the body. As we grow and develop, this etheric substance is gradually broken down between each chakra point one by one from the base upwards. The path that brings one to consider the sort of spiritual growth witchcraft has to offer, as with other traditions, should have opened the energy flows through the first three chakra points. The aim of the first degree initiation, in this respect, is to open up the flow between the third chakra (the spleen) and the fourth (the heart). The second degree initiation works on opening the energy flow between the fourth chakra (the heart) and the fifth (the throat). The third degree initiation aims to open up the flow between the fifth chakra (the throat) and the sixth (the third eye). Once this has been attained the energy flow is then fully functional and the initiate should be in full contact with the group soul and ready to start work on even higher states of consciousness through the crown chakra and beyond.

By the time an initiate is ready for the first degree initiation, it would also be reasonable to expect that she/he has studied enough to at least be aware of most of the forms of divination, psychic skills, herb-craft, charms, spell work, healing, etc – all of which are used in the Craft, and would have at least started to work at mastering at least one of these skills.

Initiation ceremonies should generally only be conducted by a witch who has been initiated to the third degree (i.e. a High Priestess or High Priest). The initiation should be carried out by the opposite sexual gender to the initiate as the duality of male and female energy is important throughout the ways of the Craft. Under no circumstances should the initiation be conducted by the same sexual gender as the initiate, the imbalance created by such a situation would not help bring about the desired transformation and could psychically damage both initiator and initiate for a very long time.

All initiations are a symbolic death and rebirth 'consciously undertaken'. Because of this the initiate would prepare her/himself by ritually cleansing in a bath of salted water (as would be the case before any formal work). The initiate then goes to the place outside of the Circle skyclad (naked and unadorned) as one would be at birth. If the initiate is shy about appearing naked before the High Priestess or High Priest then a cloak can be used. The initiate should use this time to meditate upon the ceremony that is to follow and to consider that she/he is absolutely sure that this is the path that she/he wishes to follow. If at this stage they have any doubts they should say so and back out. Any High Priestess or High Priest worth their salt would not make anyone feel guilty or ashamed by making such a choice, indeed if there is the slightest doubt then backing out should be encouraged if not insisted upon.

I do not generally advocate witches working together naked (or 'skyclad') unless everyone in the group is thoroughly comfortable with this. Whilst I appreciate that clothing can indeed interfere to some degree with the movement of one's personal energies, so too can the naked body make one feel insecure and be a very big distraction, although it could be reasonably argued that this is a matter that should be overcome as being ashamed of one's body and seeing it simply as an object of sex is to do with the Christian concept of original sin and has no place in Wicca. Light robes (or if working outside in the cold, heavy robes and cloaks – it is important to be comfortable) with no underwear are generally perfectly adequate and can help get one's mind into the right frame. Initiation is the one exception to this – in my book – as it is a rebirth, the nakedness and any contact being something that is *strictly* of a non-sexual nature. The High Priestess and High Priest in the circle represent the Goddess and God – the spiritual and symbolic Mother and Father of creation within the rebirth theme. One should not be ashamed of one's body, and certainly be prepared to stand before the gods totally unadorned. This is important to the symbolism and part of the vital element within all these rites of passage that shows that one is prepared to enter the place between the worlds without fear in one's heart.

In any initiation ritual it is important to ensure that the Goddess and God are invited and welcomed to the Circle. As the initiation is a process of rebirth, it is important to thoroughly feel their presence throughout the ritual as it is They who are the creators and They who are taking you through the initiatory process.

SELF DEDICATION AND SELF INITIATION

If the ceremony is a simple dedication, there is no need at this stage to have prepared any of the working tools of the Craft. If it is to be a self initiation then one should already have prepared an athame, a wand, a chalice, white cords and a set of robes. Not all covens will accept self initiation, though it is usually the only choice if your path is to be solitary, but if you are later invited and choose to join a coven it would be normal to expect to be initiated into that coven.

Cast the Circle in the normal way then sit before the altar and meditate upon the path you intend to set yourself on. Consider carefully what the Goddess and God mean to you and how you hope they will manifest themselves through you and through the things that you under-take in your life.

When you are ready, stand before the altar and say: *"Lady and Lord Goddess and God, I am of you as you are of me. I* [name] *have chosen to dedicate myself to you, your work, and the Craft of the Wise. I trust that you will accept me and guide me along my chosen path, wherever it shall lead me."*

Take plenty of time to meditate again, and if you have tools that you need to consecrate then do that now. If this is a self initiation rather than a self dedication, then one should move around the Circle, starting with the East and say: *"Spirits of the East, Guardians of Air, I have dedicated myself to the Goddess and God and ask for your blessings in this work."*

Moving to the South say: *"Spirits of the South, Guardians of Fire, I have dedicated myself to the Goddess and God and ask for your blessings in this work."*

Moving to the West say: *"Spirits of the West, Guardians of Water, I have dedicated myself to the Goddess and God and ask for your blessings in this work."*

Moving to the North say: *"Spirits of the North, Guardians of Earth, I have dedicated myself to the Goddess and God and ask for your blessings in this work."*

Spend a few moments meditating with the guardians of the quarters, carefully listening to anything that comes to mind.

At the end of the ritual one can use the traditional phrase: *"Love is the Law and Love is the Bond. Merry do we meet, merry shall we part, and merry shall we meet again."*

Close the Circle in the normal way.

FORMAL DEGREE INITIATION

The following rituals are based on those devised by Gerald Gardner, largely from those used in Freemasonry – the earliest written records of which are found in Scottish Freemasonry from the 17th Century but are likely to be older. Gardner made few changes to these rituals, though obviously adapted to be suitable for a pagan orientation, and I feel that whilst modifications are also acceptable (as Wicca is a non-dogmatic path that needs to develop organically with the changing times) one should keep to the basic format and incorporate the essential elements not least of all because they have been proven to work on the psychological level and (through that) the spiritual level which is, after all, the purpose of the exercise.

FIRST DEGREE INITIATION

In Wicca a male initiates a female and vice versa. The following ritual is written as a High Priest initiating a female witch. If the initiate is male then the roles need to be reversed.

The initiate should prepare a number of items before the ceremony. These are:

1. An athame.
2. A cord, 9 feet long, white for the first degree.
3. A wand.
4. Ceremonial robes.

These items are given to the High Priest before the ceremony. They are cleansed and blessed by the High Priest and left on the altar before the initiate enters the Circle.

The initiate should also choose a name for herself. This will become her Craft name, generally known only to those within her Circle. (See chapter 12 on 'Tools of the Craft'.)

In the meantime the High Priest casts a Circle in the normal way with the altar near the centre of the circle facing North. Special care is taken in inviting the Goddess and God to attend the ritual which proceeds once their presence is thoroughly felt.

The initiate's ceremonial items are cleansed and blessed and left on the altar. If the High Priestess is present then she helps with the preparation and then stands to the North of the altar facing South throughout most of the ceremony. The High Priest then cuts a gateway in the North East of Circle and goes to where the initiate is waiting. The High Priest will require his own athame, a blindfold (preferably of black silk or cotton), a 9 foot red cord (red representing birth) and two cords made from another 9 foot red cord.

High Priest: *"Are you ready to enter the place I have prepared between the Worlds to be initiated as a witch and Priestess?"*

Initiate: *"I am."*

High Priest: *"Tell me the name you have chosen for yourself."*

The initiate tells the High Priest her chosen Craft name.

The High Priest then blindfolds the initiate. This represents the darkness entered at death. The initiates wrists are tied in the middle of a 9 foot red cord behind her/his back. The ends of the cord are then taken over the shoulders and tied in front of the neck leaving a length of cord that will later be used to guide the initiate around the Circle. The position of the initiate's arms form an upward pointing triangle. One of the shorter cords is tied around the initiate's right ankle (the ends tucked in to prevent tripping) the other cord is tied around the left knee.

High Priest: *"Your legs are now neither bound nor free."*

The High Priest guides the initiate to the gateway of the circle and opens it with his athame. The High Priest carefully holds the point of his athame against the middle of the initiate's chest.

High Priest: *"I must warn you that you might just as well rush upon my blade and perish than to enter this Circle with fear in your heart."*

Initiate: *"I have two passwords — perfect love and perfect trust."*

High Priest: *"I give you a third password — a kiss."*

The High Priest kisses the initiate on the lips and enters the Circle. The initiate takes a step forward to enter the Circle of her own free will. The High Priest then closes the gateway. The initiate is turned around three times to disorient her and then remains standing.

High Priest: *"In other religions the postulant kneels, while the Priest towers above her. On this path we are taught to be humble. I therefore kneel before you to welcome and honour you. Blessed be your feet that have brought you to this place."*

High Priest kisses right foot then left.

High Priest: *"Blessed be your knees that shall kneel before the sacred altar."*

High Priest kisses right knee then left.

High Priest: *"Blessed be your womb[47] that brings life."*

High Priest kisses womb.

High Priest: *"Blessed be your breasts formed in beauty."*

High Priest kisses right breast then left.

High Priest: *"Blessed be your lips that will utter the sacred names of our Lady and Lord."*

High Priest kisses lips and embraces initiate. The initiate is then led to stand before the Eastern quarter (usually marked with a candle).

High Priest: *"Watchers of the East, Guardians of Air, before you stands _____ [chosen name of initiate] who is ready to be initiated as a witch and Priestess. What do you say?"*

There is a short pause for the Watchers to respond if they so choose. The initiate is then led to stand before the Southern quarter.

High Priest: *"Watchers of the South, Guardians of Fire, before you stands _____ [chosen name of initiate] who is ready to be initiated as a witch and Priestess. What do you say?"*

There is a short pause for the Watchers to respond if they so choose. The initiate is then led to stand before the Western quarter.

High Priest: *"Watchers of the West, Guardians of Water, before you stands _____ [chosen name of initiate] who is ready to be initiated as a witch and Priestess. What do you say?"*

There is a short pause for the Watchers to respond if they so choose. The initiate is then led to stand before the Northern quarter.

---

[47] Phallus if the initiate is male.

High Priest: *"Watchers of the North, Guardians of Earth, before you stands _____ [chosen name of initiate] who is ready to be initiated as a witch and Priestess. What do you say?"*

There is a short pause for the Watchers to respond if they so choose. The initiate is then led to stand before the altar.

High Priest: *"Are you ready and prepared to serve our Lady and Lord, Goddess and God, as a witch and Priestess?"*

Initiate: *"I am."*

High Priest pulls initiate down to kneel before the altar. High Priest kneels next to initiate (female to left of male).

High Priest: *"You are now kneeling before our Lord and Lady, in the presence of the Mighty Ones. You must swear to serve them, according to your own free will, and to the best of your ability and never reveal the secrets of the Craft unless that person is a brother or sister of the Craft who has been properly vouched for by somebody that you know and trust."*

There is a pause for a short meditation. When the High Priest considers an appropriate amount of time has passed he stands and helps the initiate to her feet. The initiate stands facing the High Priest. The High Priest takes the anointing oil from the altar (if the High Priestess is present she passes it to the High Priest). The High Priest moistens his finger with the oil and touches the initiate above the womb, right breast, left breast and then womb again, saying:

High Priest: *"This is the symbol of a Priestess*[48] of the first degree."[49]

The oil is returned to the altar. The chalice full of red wine is then taken or passed from the altar. The chalice represents the womb of the Goddess and the wine her blood. The initiate is then anointed using the same symbol as above with the wine.

High Priest: *"I anoint you with wine."*

The chalice is returned to the altar. The initiate is then kissed by the High Priest in the same places as above.

High Priest: *"I consecrate you with my lips – _____ (chosen Craft name) Priestess and witch. Blessed Be."*

The High Priest removes the cords binding the initiate's arms and legs. The High Priest then removes the blindfold. The new Priestess is then presented with her robes, which are put on. The High Priest ties her white cords around the waist (with the ends dangling below her knees). The High Priest then presents the new Priestess with her own

---

[48] It is the same for a Priest.

[49] This symbol – the downward pointing triangle – represent the triangle formed by the pubic hair on a woman, and thus the fertility of the Goddess. There is evidence that this symbol has been used in pagan and other mystery teaching throughout history – it is also used in freemasonry which quite possibly has common roots to witchcraft.

athame and wand. The significance of the tools is explained, as are the other items on the altar. The new Priestess is then shown how to consecrate and bless her own tools.

When ready the new Priestess helps the High Priest to banish the Guardians of the elements and the High Priest opens the Circle.

SECOND DEGREE INITIATION

The Second Degree Initiation follows much the same ritual as the first, with a few small, though important, changes.

First of all, when the red cords are tied around the knee and ankle, instead of the ends being left loose they are tied together, thus signifying the bonding of the witch to the Craft. It is not necessary for a new witch name to be chosen at this initiation. The ceremony follows a similar fashion up to the point of the consecration with the sign of the second degree. Whereas in the First Degree Initiation the symbol given is that of a downward pointing triangle, in the Second Degree the symbol given is that of an inverted pentagram. This represents the interdependence of the four Elements with Spirit, whilst acknowledging that the spiritual element hasn't necessarily transcended to its final position above and in full command of the Elements. The points anointed are then phallus or womb, right breast, left hip, right hip, left breast and phallus or womb.

THIRD DEGREE INITIATION

Once again this follows a similar pattern to that of the First Degree Initiation. The bonds are tied as with the Second, but a new witch name is chosen as the initiate is to be made a High Priestess or High Priest.

The symbol of the Third Degree is an upward pointing pentacle topped by an upward pointing triangle. The upright pentagram signifies that the Spirit has properly transcended and mastered the Elements. The upwards pointing triangle signifies that the initiate has made the inner union of Goddess and God and is thus in touch with the divine. The points anointed are therefore the phallus or womb, the right foot, the left knee, the right knee, the left foot and phallus or womb, followed by the lips, left breast, right breast and finally the lips again.

A Priest is appointed a '*High Priest and Magus*' whilst a Priestess is appointed '*High Priestess and Witch Queen*'.

Following the point where the new High Priestess or High Priest are presented to the four quarters the Great Rite is enacted (see page 128).

WICCANNING

A Wiccaning is a pagan equivalent to a Christening. The main difference is that in a Wiccaning the child is not bound to the religion of its parents as it is recognised that the child has a right to choose its own path when it is old enough to do so. In a Wiccaning ceremony the child is presented to the Gods and blessings are asked for it, and the parents and any god/goddess parents are committed to protecting the child and sharing responsibility for its upbringing.

The child may have a sacred name chosen for it, which it has a choice to use or not when it becomes old enough to decide for itself. The ceremony should be conducted by a High Priestess and High Priest. If the child is a girl then the High Priest takes the main role within the ceremony and if the child is a boy then the High Priestess takes the main role. The following ceremony is written as if it were a High Priest presenting a girl, it can easily be transposed to be that of a High Priestess presenting a boy.

Any presents for the child are placed on the altar which should be decorated with plenty of bright colours, preferably flowers. The Circle is cast whilst the parents, child and any other guests wait outside of the area to the North-East. The High Priest cuts an entrance in the North-East and welcomes in everyone who stand around within the Circle wherever they please. Parents and child stand before the altar facing the High Priest and High Priestess. If there are too many guests to fit in the Circle they will need to remain outside and observe from there. Any God parents obviously need to be within the Circle.

High Priest: *"We have met in this Circle to ask for the blessing of the Goddess and God on* [name of child] *the daughter of* [name of mother] *and* [name of father] *so that she may grow in beauty and strength, in joy and in wisdom. There are many paths to follow and we must all choose our own, we therefore do not bind* [name of child] *to the path of her parents as she is too young to choose, but we ask the Goddess and God, who know all the paths and to whom all paths lead, to bless, protect and prepare her through her formative years so that when she is ready she shall know without doubt or fear which path is hers so that she can walk it boldly and with love in her heart."*

The mother hands the young child to the High Priest.

[50]High Priest: *"*[name of mother], *does your child also have a sacred name?"*

Mother: *"Her sacred name is - - - - ."*

---

[50] If a sacred name is not used then this is missed out and the ordinary given name is used throughout.

The High Priest marks a pentagram on the child's forehead with oil.[51] "*I anoint you* [ordinary name] *with oil and give you the sacred name of* [sacred name]."

The High Priest marks a pentagram on the child's head with wine. "*I anoint you* [sacred name] *with wine in the name of the God.*"

The High Priest marks a pentagram on the child's head with water. "*I anoint you* [sacred name] *with water in the name of the Goddess.*"

High Priest: "*Watchers of the East, South, West and North, we bring before you* [ordinary name], *who is also known as* [sacred name] *who has been properly anointed within this Circle. Hear now that she is under the protection of our Lady and Lord, the Goddess and God.*"

High Priest: "*I call upon our God to give this child the gift of strength.*"

High Priestess: "*I call upon our Goddess to give this child the gift of beauty*".

High Priest: "*I call upon our God to give this child the gift of wisdom.*"

High Priestess: "*I call upon our Goddess to give this child the gift of love.*"

High Priest: "*Are there two within the Circle who will stand as godparents to* [child's ordinary name]?"

The godparents step forward to stand next to the mother and father of the child.

The High Priest asks the Godmother: "*Do you promise to be a friend to* [child's ordinary name] *throughout her childhood, to aid and guide her whenever needed in concordance with her parents. Do you promise to watch over her and love her as if she was of your own blood until by the grace of our Lord and Lady she is ready to choose her own path?*"

Godmother says: "*I do.*"

High Priestess then asks the same question of the Godfather who replies in the same way.

High Priest: "*The Goddess and God have blessed this child, the Mighty Ones of the Elements have acknowledged her and we her friends have welcomed her. May the light always shine on* [child's ordinary name] *who is also known as* [sacred name]. *So it must be.*"

All reply: "*So it must be*".

The gifts for the child are then presented to her. The High Priestess then cuts a gateway in the Circle and all leave except her and the High Priest. The Circle is then closed in the normal way. Drinking and feasting follows in an informal manner as befits such an occasion.

---

[51] It is important that a very light anointing oil is used as a child's skin is very sensitive.

172

HANDFASTING

A pagan handfasting is the equivalent of the Christian marriage ceremony. Traditionally the couple make pledges to each other that are kept for a year and a day, after which they are reaffirmed or they are handparted. More often, however, couples choose to bond for more of an indefinite period more often intending a life bond more akin to the Christian ceremony. Advice would normally be sought from the High Priestess and High Priest chosen to work the ceremony. Ultimately it should be the choice of the couple. They may decide that a year and a day is a realistic commitment, after which they can reaffirm their vows to each other, or they may be so confident that they wish to bond for a longer period. Either is acceptable as long as the vows they make to each other are sincere.

One of the beauties of handfasting is that the ceremony has only a loose structure and can be adapted to include the words and other elements as chosen by the couple being handfasted. As with all rituals, feel free to use the words that follow, adapt them, or completely write your own as you think appropriate, though remembering to incorporate the obvious vital elements in some form.

Handfasting is naturally a joyous occasion, so whilst there are obviously serious elements to it, especially the pledges made between the couple, and the bonding itself, try to keep the ceremony light and cheerful. Whilst it is a private matter between the couple and their gods, bringing plenty of guests to witness the handfasting, and having a joyous celebration afterwards helps to put energy into the ceremony which can only help strengthen the bond.

Altar in centre of circle. On it seasonal flowers and fruit. Two white candles. Taper. Consecrated water and incense. Consecrated cakes and wine. Rings on cushion. 2ft length of ribbon – white. Gifts appropriate to the elements can be placed in front of the quarter candles if wished as mementoes of the occasion. A traditional broom is also used at the end of the ceremony and needs to be leaning against the altar from the start.

The Circle is cast in the normal way.

The High Priest goes to the East and cuts an opening in the Circle (using three sweeps of his athame). The Bride and Groom enter in the East, led by sponsors and followed by other circle participants. When all have entered the High Priest seals the Circle behind them. The Bride's sponsor may scatter petals around the Circle and especially where the Bride and Groom are to stand. They walk around the circle deosil (clockwise) and come to a rest before the altar (facing East).

High Priestess says: *"We stand in a place between the Worlds that has been consecrated and sealed before the Goddess and the God and the elements of the four quarters. Welcome"*.

High Priestess turns to the bride and groom and says: *"Welcome [groom's name]* and *[bride's name]* to this Circle, cast as a place where you will be joined in body and in spirit".*

The High Priestess and High Priest take the couple to stand before the candle marking the Eastern Quarter.

High Priest says: *"Watchers of the East – Guardians of Air we call on you to grant your blessings to this couple in the form of optimism, wisdom, and joy."*

Couple say: *"Blessed be Spirits of the East."*

All move to the South:

High Priest says: *"Watchers of the South – Guardians of Fire, we call on you to grant your blessings to this couple in the form of courage, loyalty and strength".*

Couple say: *"We thank you Spirits of the South".*

All move to the West.

High Priestess says: *"Watchers of the West – Guardians of Water, we call on you to grant your blessings to this couple in the form of love, devotion and tranquillity".*

Couple say: *"We thank you Spirits of the West".*

All move to the North.

High Priestess says: *"Watchers of the North – Guardians of Earth, we call on you to grant your blessings to this couple in the form of strength, responsibility and fertility."*

Couple say: *"We thank you spirits of the North".*

All return to the altar with the Bride and Groom facing East and the High Priestess and High Priest facing them from the other side of the altar.

High Priestess says: *"Goddess of beauty and form, Mother of the fertile Earth, we ask that you witness and protect these rites. Bless and keep this union in heart and in spirit".*

High Priest says: *"God of creation and power, who warms our hearts through the midday Sun, we ask that you witness and protect these rites. Bless and keep this union in heart and in spirit."*

High Priestess says: *"We stand at the centre of the circle where all things meet their opposite. God and Goddess, Masculine and Feminine, Darkness and Light, Spirit and Matter. These things make each whole and complete, just as you [Bride's name]* and *you [Groom's name]* are to join together, two halves that make a whole. You must not enter this union lightly. You will swear your commitment to each other before the Goddess and God and the Mighty Spirits of the Quarters who have blessed this union. Hold true to each other as you hold true your values and beliefs."*

High Priest says: *"This is not the first cycle of your lives together. Rather than start anew, this ceremony represents to you both a new season. Just as spring*

174

is a time of planting and summer is a time of growth, this cycle represents the harvest of growth, maturity and respect That which you have learnt in your lives to this day shall nourish this harvest, providing a rich and stable place from which to grow together as the cycle of life continues".

Priestess says: "*Who here supports this man and offers their friendship and love to this union?*"

Groom's sponsor steps forward to the side of the groom and says: "*I do.*"

High Priestess says: (turning to Groom)

' [Groom's name], *is it your wish to take* [Bride's name]'*s hand to be your partner, to join together your heart with hers, uniting your spirit with hers; endowing her with your trust, respect and love?*"

Groom answers: "*It is.*"

High Priest says: "*Who here supports this woman and offers their friendship and love to this union?*"

Brides sponsor steps forward to the side of the bride and says: "*I do.*"

High Priest says: (turning to Bride)

"[Bride's name], *is it your wish to take* [Groom's name]'*s hand to be your partner, to join together your heart with his, uniting your spirit with his; endowing him with your trust, respect and love?*"

Bride answers: "*It is.*"

High Priest now says: "*A ring is an unbroken circle, a symbol of unity and love, representative of the circle here within which you make your vows.*" Addressing the Grooms sponsor "*Please present the rings*".

The groom takes the ring cushion and holds it before the High Priestess.

High Priestess says: "*Goddess and God, in Divine Union, we ask for your blessings upon these rings*".

The Grooms sponsor presents the cushion to the Groom and he takes the Brides ring.

High Priest says: "*Will you* [Bride's name] *accept this ring as a loving symbol of* [Groom's name] *vows this day?*"

Bride answers: "*I will.*"

Groom takes the ring and places it on the Brides finger saying: "*With this ring I offer you a reminder of our strength together, and the vision we share, for a life that begins and ends with love and understanding.*"

The grooms sponsor gives the cushion to the High Priestess. She presents it to the High Priest who in turn presents it to the Bride's sponsor. The Bride's sponsor takes the cushion and offers it to the Bride who takes the Grooms ring.

High Priestess says: "*Will you* [Groom's name] *accept this ring as a loving symbol of* [Bride's name] *vows this day?*"

Groom answers: "*I will*".

Bride takes the ring and places it on groom's finger saying: "With this ring I offer you a reminder of our strength together, and the vision we share, for a life that begins and ends with love and understanding"

Bride and groom now join left hands – bride's hand on the top of the groom's. The High Priestess takes the white ribbon and loosely drapes it over the groom's wrist saying: "[Groom's name], *please give your vows to* [Bride's name]."

Groom says:[52] "*I ask you* [Bride's name], *to join with me as my partner. I give you my pledge that I shall love you and honour you as I love the Goddess and God themselves. I pledge that I shall always be honest, faithful and committed to you through good times and bad, and that I shall do everything within my power to ensure your life is full of the joys and freedom of life with respect for your needs today and always".*

High Priestess loosely drapes the ribbon over the bride's wrist and says to bride: "[Bride's name], *please give your vows to* [Groom's name]..."

Bride says:[53] "*I ask you* [Groom's name], *to join with me as my partner. I give you my pledge that I shall love you and honour you as I love the Goddess and God themselves. I pledge that I shall always be honest, faithful and committed to you through good times and bad, and that I shall do everything within my power to ensure your life is full of the joys and freedom of life with respect for your needs today and always".*

Priestess ties the lover's knot and says: "*As I tie this knot I bind the vows and pledges you have made to each other. Gentle are the bonds of this Union. Let the powers of the Spirit guide you, let the strength of your wills bind you together, let the power of love and desire make you happy, and the strength of your dedication make you inseparable. Let your spirits support and strengthen each other so that you may experience all of the joys of life together.*"

High Priest says: "*Throughout this rite, within this Circle, you have both been joined in Body and in Spirit. The knot is a symbol of your spiritual ties, the rings are the symbols of your physical bonds. As the God and Goddess witness these rites, you are now joined before them.*"

The Bride and Groom now kiss.

The Priestess now helps the Bride and Groom to slip their hands out of the lover's knot without untying it and hands the knot to the Bride. The knot should form a bow. She hands it to her sponsor for safekeeping.

The High Priest turns to altar and picks up the plate of cakes saying: "*These cakes are baked from the seed that represents our God.*"

---

[52] The vows should be written by the Bride and Groom. These vows are given as an example.

[53] The vows should be written by the Bride and Groom. These vows are given as an example.

The High Priest offers the plate to the Bride who takes a cake. The High Priest says: *"From this day* [Bride's name]*, you shall know the God through* [Groom's name]*."*

The Bride eats the cake and takes a second which she feeds to the Groom. The High Priest then takes the plate around everyone in the Circle who each take a cake and eat it, offering one to the High Priestess before taking one himself.

The High Priestess turns to altar and picks up the chalice full of wine and says to the Groom: *"As a symbol of* [Bride's name] *I offer this wine which represents the blood of the Goddess"*.

The High Priestess offers a sip to the Groom saying: *"From this day* [Groom's name]*, shall you know the Goddess through* [Bride's name]*."*

The Groom takes the chalice and offers a sip to the Bride and then hands it back to the High Priestess who takes it around the Circle for everyone to take a sip finally coming to the High Priest who then takes the chalice and offers a sip to the High Priestess.

High Priest addresses the group and says: *"We entered this place in perfect love and perfect trust, may we leave it also in perfect love and perfect trust so that this couple may start there bonding together as they mean to continue. May their lives together be full of joy and happiness, and may the Goddess and God provide all that they require to grow together in peace and harmony and give them the strength to support each other through all the trials this life brings. So it must be."*

All say: *"So it mote be."*

The High Priestess takes the broom and moves to the East where she lays it on the ground and then cuts a gateway with her athame. The Bride and Groom jump the broom together and leave the Circle, followed by all the others besides the High Priestess and High Priest.

The Circle is closed in the normal way. There follows plenty of feasting and fun.

OTHER RITES OF PASSAGE

Other rites of passage have already been discussed in this book, such as those important stages in the development of a child or a young adult such as entering puberty. There are other stages in the process of a life where we experience important milestones that deserve to be marked, such as entering middle age, old age and the final transition – death. Croning, for instance, is the transition into the latter stages of one's life along with all the wisdom and knowledge built up in that life, is one of the milestones marked particularly within Wicca, not least of all because of its relationship with the triple Goddess aspects.

Ceremonies and rituals can be designed to mark these rites of passage. They do, however, demand a great deal of personal input and any attempt to provide a standard form would be futile. For a Wiccan, working in a Circle between the Worlds and invoking the spiritual guardians of the elements tends to be a natural way of doing things. What is performed and takes place between the general framework is for each individual or group to determine.

I reached one such milestone at my fortieth birthday. To me it felt far more than another birthday, it felt like a transition into middle age, and I felt compelled to mark it with something personal and spiritual. The physical life of a man can be related to a wheel not dissimilar to the wheel of a year. If one considers that one enters the wheel of life between North and East (as one enters a cast Circle) then the first stage of one's life is the spring (associated with East); the second as one reaches maturity is the summer (associated with summer and in a male the warrior phase); the third as one reaches middle age is the autumn (associated with West and the poet phase); and finally the winter in old age (North and prophet phase). At the age of forty I felt I was moving from South into West, from warrior to poet phase, and the following prayer was devised to mark the occasion and was conducted within a cast Circle. I provide it merely as an example...

My Lady, my Lord, Goddess and God,
I [magic name], am your witch, mage and priest.
I am of you, as you are of me.

I stand before you today,
Between the Watchers of the South and West,
As the wheel turns in this life of mine.

For me the wheel turns from Summer to Autumn,
And I transform from warrior to poet,
Entering and welcoming the evening time of this life.

Grant me the grace to accept the turning of the wheel,
To welcome the maturity that it brings,
So that I may continue our work and honour your names.

You have taught me to walk lightly on this earth,
To take no more than I need,
To give and return rather than practise greed.

May I use the wisdom you have given me,
As I continue to grow and learn,
To maintain harmony between us and those around me.

Your flames burn bright on the altar of my heart,
To provide the light I need to see the mistakes I have made,
And find the humility to recognise and admit my failings.

I have the right to be as I am, and better than I am,
To be strong in body, mind and spirit,
And to bow my head to none other than you.

My Lady, my Lord, Goddess and God,
I step from the fire into the water,
As my love for you burns it shall now flow.

For the good of all,
So mote it be.

19

WORKING MAGIC AND
HOW MAGIC WORKS

Before anything can be manifested on the physical plane it needs to have first been manifested in thought on another plane. Magic therefore involves developing a relationship with those other planes, through visualisation, expanding consciousness into the other planes and bringing back the necessary material for the original thought to manifest on the physical. That is magic. The thought form, however, may have come from some materialistic or egotistic desire that serves no deep purpose other than self-gratification. On the other hand, the thought form may not have been projected from the lower self, but from the Higher Self, or even from spiritual entities outside of the Self. If working with such forces the work then becomes what is commonly known as high magic and is most readily achievable through working 'between the Worlds' in a situation that is necessarily ritualistic.

There are many forms of magic, and none more valid than any other. To ensure that ritual magic truly works it is necessary to be self-disciplined and put in a great deal of work through daily meditation and practice. Anyone who thinks they can simply buy a book of spells and expect them to work effectively without having trained themselves to concentrate, focus and visualise, as well as have a strong personal understanding of the astral, elemental and spiritual dimensions is going to be extremely disappointed. Magic, whether it be ritual or folk magic, works on the physical plane as well as the other dimensions.

Utilising a herb for instance will use the physical elements of the herb, but used in conjunction with a healing visualisation of any depth, starts working on the astral, elemental and spiritual planes as well through both the practitioner and the various correspondences of the herb used. To what degree this healing is successful depends on how adept the practitioner is, the clarity or sincerity of the visualisation and the appropriate herb. A healing application such as this may well fall under the categories of herbalism or folk magic, or more accurately a combination of the two. Ritual magic works in much the same way although a more formal and thorough approach is applied.

Many people fear magic because they do not understand it, or how it works. It can appear frightening because it works with forces that are unseen or hidden from the uninitiated. Occult means 'hidden' and it is not until that which is hidden is understood and recognised that the magician can manipulate these unseen forces. The Wiccan saying 'in perfect love and perfect trust'[54] refers to more than the initiate's feelings towards the High Priestess, High Priest, and others that they may work with. The initiate needs to overcome fear of the previously unknown and open themselves up to the greater realities and all that is possible within that greater reality.

I would strongly urge anyone starting to work magic that they fully understand everything they do before it is tried out. To approach magic with fear in one's heart is a folly. As I have said earlier in this book, witchcraft is foremost a religious practice and a method of self-development. Start off by using ritual to connect with nature as the wheel of the year turns, it is through the faith and understanding that this builds that one can start to move forward and begin to use the energy generated by and connection with nature – the seen and unseen. Do NOT expect to pick up a book like this and start working deep ritual magic. Whilst some may take to it quickly, for others several years of hard inner work could be involved.

To understand how magic works it is necessary to build an understanding of the planes of existence that exist beyond that which is experienced by the five physical human sense; first to experience it with the relational side of the brain, then to rationalise it into the conscious. The Higher Self is reached through the sub-conscious and a thorough and sound relationship with the Higher Self can only be achieved through self-development, balancing oneself with the elements within, delving deep into the inner realms with a certain degree of objectivity and making the necessary adjustments. It is the Higher Self that is the complete soul of each individual – the 'grail' and gateway through which the other normally unseen planes are reached. There are many stories throughout the ages and throughout cultures that describe the search for the 'grail'. The analogies usually describe a search for a physical object that is never found in the material world because it can only truly be found within.[55]

Ritual magic is worked 'between the worlds'. One is working both on the physical plane and beyond on the astral, elemental planes and

---

[54] 'Perfect love' and 'perfect trust' are two of the three passwords used in Wiccan initiation ceremonies, the third being a kiss.

[55] There are some particularly materialist people who claim to have found the 'holy grail' as a physical object. One such example can be found at Chalice Well Gardens in Glastonbury and is actually a (some might say gaudy) piece of Italian pottery. However, having said that, Chalice Well Gardens is certainly a powerful energy centre and an ideal place to connect with nature and the inner self through meditation, so those heading there to find the 'grail' may well end up finding it anyway.

spiritual planes. The circle that is cast creates a space that is between these planes of existence. You are working not for yourself, though your own development is a vital element, but for the greater good and the benefit of the will of the gods of which we are each an element. You will get to a stage in your spiritual development (if you work hard and sincerely) where you realise that they (the gods) are of you as you are of them. You will also realise that even if you are working a ritual on your own, you are not really alone. Having placed yourself between the worlds you are working with all sorts of spirits and elementals in partnership with them and not always for a purpose purely of your own devising. Once the channels have been fully opened we begin to realise that our will is guided by a higher intelligence that has a specific purpose which is to grow through experience and thus, as an integral element of the divine spirit, contributing to the overall growth of the divine and its inevitable project to bring the various planes of existence into harmony.

Working a ritual through ceremony helps to focus the mind and all the senses on the work at hand. Through it you will be creating a thought form, or entity, that will build according to the energy put into it. Additional energy will be put into the invocation if you are working with others who share similar values to you and who work with similar symbolism.

In order to focus one's mind on the work at hand, thorough preparation can do a great deal to help. First of all consider exactly what it is you aim to achieve. Consider the moral aspects of the work you intend to do. The supposed Wiccan law that suggests non-manipulation as a tenet is not always entirely possible in the face of many real situations, but you must consider all possibilities and protect yourself if necessary. For example, if a friend is being stalked by a stranger, or even a jealous ex-partner looking for revenge, it is difficult to offer protection without some manipulation of the stalker even though the work is likely to end up being 'for the good of all'. 'If it harm none, do what you will' is the Wiccan law introduced by Gerald Gardner, a very much misunderstood term and one which seems to have little bearing historically. The law is not intended to encourage carte-blanche anarchism for each individual to manifest what they need materially as long as it doesn't affect anybody, but relates to a much deeper sense of 'will' being that which is one's purpose in this life. It is a law that I believe has been much misunderstood in our days of fluffy new ageism.

One of the great strengths of the Celtic tribes was undoubtedly their sense of community. In order to protect one's own community it is often the case that some form of defence is put up, be that physically, psychic or both. There is white magic and black magic, and one must carefully consider the karmic come-backs as necessary, but many situations when thoroughly considered tend to be somewhat grey. 'There are four types

182

of witch – black, grey, white and publicity.'[56] (Personally I have little time for the black or publicity witches and feel they are best left alone to play their own games and learn the hard way.) Protecting one's own community – and that community can be a circle of friends who are not necessarily living in the same part of the world – is something that I consider to be a worthy part of one's esoteric work as long as it negates interference with each other's own life course. It is necessary to consider the Wiccan three-fold law which I do consider entirely valid. Whatever one does returns three times over. It does so when working esoterically because one works in the other planes of existence and therefore the work done on the physical plane affects the astral, the elemental and the spiritual.

You also need to consider whether the work you are doing, if it is for oneself, is for a *real* need and not simply some form of materialistic or egotistical gratification. The maxim I work to in such situations is NEED not GREED. If you work continually for materialistic or egotistical gratification you are merely falling into the trap that so many fall into, that of pandering to a glamour, and have failed to fully connect with one's divine will. The magic may at first appear to have some effect, but one will find that the three-fold law pays back in some particularly vicious ways. The spirits do not respond well to those who work for greed.

The next thing to consider is how you are going to focus on your objective. The more symbolism you use within the ritual, the easier you will find it to focus your attention on the work, and the easier you will find it to work between the planes.

I would emphasise here that in ritual magic incorporating the four elements (plus the fifth 'spirit') is essential, though there are occasions, when a matter of balance is required, when one of the four elements is used more then the others. The four elements correspond to the four quarters in a magic circle. Water (west) and Earth (north) are considered female energies; Fire (south) and Air (east) male energies. Also for reasons of balance work tends to be that much stronger with male and female energies working together within the Circle.

There are many items that can be used within the ritual (see also chapter 12 on *Tools of the Craft*). An appropriate mixture of coloured candles, herbal mixtures or incense, crystals, ritual tools, poppets, talismen must be carefully considered and pre-prepared. By appropriate mixture I mean not only the herbs and crystals, etc, that correspond most closely to the work at hand, but also introducing within the work the four elements. By using tools that appeal to all of your physical senses you strengthen the ability to focus and concentrate on the work you have undertaken.

---

[56] Quote from Robert Cochrane.

I have increasingly found it difficult to offer more than a general idea of what is involved in such a magical working. When dealing with specific situations there are never two sets of circumstances that are identical. For this reason I have included in this book various tables of correspondences for you to introduce the appropriate elements into your own work in addition to a few of the basic rituals. The best way for me to explain a ritual working is by example, from which I hope you will see how the elements are incorporated and how this aids the work at hand. Some rituals are more elaborate than others. Some work directly on the subconscious through psychology reaching the inner self on the edge of the astral plane, others work through this same route to deeper levels. What follows are four examples starting with the simpler ritual and gradually becoming more elaborate:

EXAMPLE 1 – SIMPLE CANDLE SPELL

Candle magic is a daily routine for any witch. Refer to the colour correspondences in the appendices to pick the appropriate colour candles. There are many elaborate variations to candle spells utilising all sorts of different colour correspondences as well as metal pins that are charged and stuck into the side of the candles.

There is no real need to cast a thorough Circle, but if you feel the need to do so then that is fine. Choose a candle of the most appropriate colour depending on the work you are undertaking. If the spell is one for healing, then you might want to choose a blue candle for example. If you want to put passion and strength into the spell you may well use a red candle.

Using your consecrating oil, take the candle and dab a few drops of oil on it. Visualise what you hope to achieve as the candle burns. Using your hands, spread the oil over all of the candle saying:

> *"Lord and Lady, Goddess and God, I consecrate this candle in your name. With your blessing I call upon you to aid me in my work. So it must be."*

Light the candle and leave it to burn safely away to nothing on your altar. Sit in front of it for as long as possible using meditation and visualisation techniques to bring about whatever you are working for.

EXAMPLE 2 – SIMPLE KNOT SPELL

Cast a Circle in the normal way before going to bed. Clearly visualise whatever it is that you intend to manifest in your life and ensure that you concentrate on this throughout the knot tying procedure. The piece of string needs to be around twelve inches long at least.

1. Perform the spell at midnight with a new piece of string, alone in a candle-lit room.
2. Have incense burning.
3. Get very clearly in your mind what you wish for. Concentrate and banish all other thoughts.
4. After tying the ninth knot, pass the string through the smoke of the incense, snuff out the candles and go to bed.
5. Put the string under your pillow.
6. Carry the cord with you (in your pocket) but don't let anyone see it (except another witch).
7. Don't talk about the wish.

The first knot is tied at one end of the piece of string, the second at the other end, the third in the middle, the fourth half way between the first and third, the fifth half way between the third and second, the sixth, seventh, eighth and ninth half way between these.

By the knot of one,
The spell's begun.
By the knot of two,
It comes true.
By the knot of three,
It shall be.
By the knot of four,
It's strengthened more.
By the knot of five,
May it thrive.
By the knot of six,
The spell we fix.
By the knot of seven,
The stars of the heavens.
By the knot of eight,
The hand of fate.
By the knot of nine,
It is mine!

EXAMPLE 3 – THE MODERATELY ELABORATE

A pregnant friend of mine was rushed into hospital experiencing labour pains. Being three months premature it was clearly important to send healing to help complement the work of the doctors and nurses in reducing the contractions and giving energy as well as protection to all those involved. Ideally I would have cast a thorough circle, having prepared myself with a ritual bath, etc, but the situation demanded some urgency. Therefore I prepared a few tools, crystals and incense mixtures before my altar and quickly cast a circle using my athame[57].

Having meditated briefly, calling on the Goddess and God and names of the god elements I most frequently associate (a matter of personal choice) I started a visualisation whilst preparing the physical representation of the work I was doing before me, which helped the focus. Having lit the central altar candle (representing the one source) I then lit the Goddess and God candles which stand to the rear of the altar on either side. A chalice full of water was already on the altar. I then lit a stick of patchouli incense (good I find for representing love and calming when working and visualisation). I also lit a lump of charcoal and started burning two special herbal incense mixtures[58] then picked a number of crystals that were cleansed in the smoke. I had already, therefore, introduced fire (candles), water (in the chalice representing the womb), air (incense) and earth (crystals). My constant visualisation and call to the deities bringing in the element of spirit. I chose quite a large number of crystals – I am fortunate in having built up quite a collection – and for this occasion I decided to use a large number of amethysts (good for general healing); a few rose quartz crystals (for love); carnelian (for strength); a lapis lazuli (healing and calm); as well as a few large clear quartz crystals (just to add extra energy for good measure). These I placed carefully in a circle around the altar candle whilst seeing my pregnant friend surrounded by healing energy and calm.

I then took another small chalice, placing it to the left of the altar candle and put a small lit candle inside it. This was to represent the unborn child alive in the womb. This I joined to the altar candle by means of placing a large rose quartz wand pointing from the chalice to the altar candle to help signify the link between mother and child and keep the bond strong. The small chalice was then surrounded by more amethyst and clear quartz crystals for good measure, and specifically to protect the little child. Finally I took a large, long-burning red candle (for strength) which was consecrated with oil and lit. This last candle

---

[57] It is important to keep this circle visualised at the back of one's mind throughout – this comes with practice. It is not always necessary to physically cast a full circle, mark the quarters with candles and call upon the elemental guardians, though when there is time to do this it frees the mind up for the rest of the work to a certain degree.

[58] In this case a special Goddess (Cerridwen) and God (Cernnunos) bought pre-mixed from a shop in Glastonbury.

was to remain burning for as long as possible throughout the night, next day and following night to keep the continuity going and to help keep my mind focused on sending what I could not just for the mother and unborn child, but also for her husband and family who were also stressed to say the least.

At the end I took myself into a deep meditation, and – with athame in hand (used to direct my will) – called on my spirit guides and helpers to aid me in my work in supporting everyone concerned. After a lengthy session I thanked the gods and spirits, opened the circle I had kept around me throughout, but kept returning to the altar for a quick five-minute additional burst.

I hope you can see throughout this ritual how I used every element in a specific way to help both visualise the necessary healing, but also through meditation (astral) and calling on the gods and spirit guides (elemental and spiritual) I ensured the work was carried through on all the different planes of existence as best I could. The symbology of the items being used on the altar helped me connect with my sub-conscious mind (that works in symbols) and through this function I worked on the astral and spiritual levels through meditation. The energies of the herbs (and the rising smoke) the burning candles and the crystals also help the connection on different levels from the physical to the elemental.

With doctors and nurses working with drugs in the hospital, my work, and a number of other friends called in to send energy in their own way, the outcome was that by the morning the contractions had slowed considerably. Mother and still unborn child were moved to a quieter ward to continue the recovery.

Had there been more time I would have cast a more thorough circle between the worlds and even spent time picking some appropriate fresh herbs. There are times when it is better to make do with what one has around them at the time – to adapt and compromise.

EXAMPLE 4 – WORKING FOR THE GREATER GOOD

The following is a ritual that I conducted during the height of the civil war in the former Yugoslavia soon before UN and Nato troops decided finally to intervene and take positive action. It was conducted in a special circle on top of a sacred hill near Honiton in Devon, the site of an ancient Iron Age hill fort. It was conducted alone, though my High Priestess worked the ritual at the same time as I did from her home where she linked in with me to give it extra energy and balance.

Cast the circle in the normal way – use a black altar candle to absorb and banish negativity. Once the circle has been sealed, the quarters called and the Gods welcomed, stand with your chalice filled with spring water. Place a moonstone in the chalice and hold it up to the moon. Try to hold it in the position whereby you can see Her light flowing into the chalice. Ask that She charge the water with healing energy and then drink it. Visualise the healing energy flowing through every atom in your body.

'Cernunnos, Cerridwen, Ogma, Rhiannon, Dana – I am your witch and your Priest.

'I call upon you to aid me in my work to invoke the love, and understanding that is required to end the violence in the Balkans. I call for the light of mediation and conciliation to balance the darkness of hatred, bloodshed and destruction.'

Take rolled-up newspaper cutting and hold it over the altar candle. Meditate and tune in to the energies working for peace.

'As this report burns, it sheds the light needed to end the violence in and around Yugoslavia. As the smoke rises, the darkness is dissolved.'

Whilst it burns, focus on it, 'send' your healing and once it is all ash, sprinkle with frankincense oil.

'Cerridwen, as Mother Goddess, embrace and heal those who are out of balance with their feminine aspects, and help them to find a way to restore that balance.

'Diana, as you glow so bright, bring light to the hearts of those on both sides of this conflict to see a way forward that avoids further violence and restores peace.'

Holding a rose quartz crystal in your left hand, face East, and symbolically point the athame to the Balkans. Concentrate on the final outcome of this work but don't send yet. Standing in the God position send, using also all that healing energy that you have charged yourself with from the chalice. Visualise the positive peaceful energy flowing from your blade, and ask that the Gods direct it to the Balkans.

At the same time as sending, also draw from the earth, and from the energy that will also be being sent to you. Remember to retain some energy for yourself else you will be drained and ill.

Place both your hands on the earth (lying down is better) and just keep contact with the earth for a few minutes. This 'earths' you and also replenishes you.

'Lady and Lord, Goddess and God, and all those who have helped put energy into this ritual, I thank you for aiding me in my work, and protecting

me. May the peace that is resolved be everlasting and help bring perfect fulfilment to all involved. So it must be!'

Clear the circle in the normal way.

RAISING THE CONE OF POWER

In the chapter on basic circle casting we learnt that the Circle is actually a sphere within which we create a place 'between the worlds'. The sphere that we create obviously must be large enough for us to carry out our work. I find a nine-feet diameter Circle just about ideal for one or two people. Much smaller than this and one would not be able to stand in the bulk of the Circle without breaking its barrier and thus destroying the energy that one requires to keep the Circle where it is.

However, we need to consider the way the energies flow in a fully cast Circle. It is not enough simply to cast one's athame around the circumference and then let the Circle do its own thing. The energy comes from the witch and the Circle will only remain whilst the witch maintains the astral visualisation. It should also be noted that the energy within the sphere of power is not static, but a continuous flow of spiralling energies. Having created the workspace we have created a place between the four elements of the quarters, to the East, South, West and North, as well as the energies from above and below. Those energies do not just stand there, but swirl together as we work and,

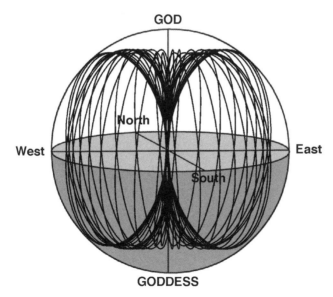

▲ *Figure 17 – The energy spiraling through the Circle between the Elements and the gods.*

189

when working magic, we gradually build the momentum up to a crescendo, releasing the energy to where it is required through a focal point known as the 'Cone of Power'.

The Cone of Power can be raised in various ways, most commonly using a mixture of chant, music and movement or dance.

Having prepared the elements one is using for the magic and through ritual become thoroughly focused one builds up the power, whilst keeping the focus firmly in mind. Once the power is raised, ideally when it is at its peak, the energy is suddenly released towards its target. You will both feel the energy being raised, swirling around the Circle, and you will feel the release which can leave one feeling quite drained. It is after this sort of work that one thoroughly appreciates the need and benefit for grounding.

If working alone one can work using physical movement and dance, utilising chant and/or music, or one can work entirely in meditation on the astral plane without any physical movement. You will find through practice what works best for you. The use of chants can be particularly strong if using something with a simple, strong rhythm. The subconscious responds well to rhythm – it is why one may sometimes find the mind continually churning through a song that was heard on the radio or in a shop, even when it is a song that one is not particularly keen on.

If working in a group, one can also work either using physical chant and dance, completely on the astral, or a mixture of the two. Normally the High Priestess, or someone else chosen for the task, will place themselves in the centre of the action gathering the swirling energy together. When she or he feels the energy has risen to an appropriate pitch a signal is given and everyone stops and drops to the ground whilst the Cone of Power is sent to its target.

FINAL WORD ON MAGIC

One final word on working magic, and a very important one. Do not, under any circumstances, think you can read and study this book, any other book, or any number of books for that matter, and presume that you can start working magic straight away. I could hand you some sheet music and a CD of Bach. You could see the notes on the page, and hear the music on the CD, but it would be a long time before you could sit before an instrument, play it, and do it justice. Spells do not work just by saying the right words and using the appropriate tools. Magic can take years of intense study and practice before you become an adept. There is absolutely no substitute for hard and sincere work. If you try to fly before you grow wings you will most likely have a serious and hard-hitting fall.

20

APPENDICES

I have given brief descriptions of many, though not all, of the British and Irish Celtic goddesses and gods. There are many more to be found throughout the former Celtic lands that once covered much of Europe and even more in other pagan traditions too numerous to mention here, though many of them have similar correspondences.

CELTIC GODDESSES

ANA
(Irish.) Also known as Anann and Anu. Great Goddess of all goddesses. Earth Goddess of fertility and plenty. Sometimes an aspect in a goddess trinity with Babd and Macha as the Goddess of fate known collectively as the Morrigan.

ARIANRHOD
(Welsh.) Goddess of the Silver Wheel (of stars) associated with the full moon. Goddess of reincarnation and fertility. Sometimes the mother aspect in a goddess trinity. Mother of Lleu Llaw Gyffes and sister to Gwydion.

BADB
(Irish.) Also known as Cauth Bodva (Gaulish). Mother aspect of a goddess trinity with Ana and Macha. Sister of Macha, Morrigan and Ana (see Ana). Goddess of the cauldron of life, wisdom and enlightenment. Also known as a war goddess.

BANBA
(Irish.) An aspect in a goddess trinity with Fotia and Eriu. One of the three queens of the Tuatha de Danaan, the daughters of the Dagda.

BLODEUWEDD

(Welsh.) Also known as Blodwin, Blancheflower or 'flower-face'. Made from the flowers of the oak, broom and meadowsweet by the gods Math and Gwydion as a wife for Lleu to whom she was unfaithful. Sometimes the maiden aspect of a goddess trinity. Goddess of flowers, wisdom and initiations.

BOANN

(Irish.) Goddess of the River Boyne. Mother of Aengus mac Og with the Dagda. Related to Samhain as this is the date supposed to mark Boann and the Dagda's mating, though the same date marks his mating with the Morrigan.

BRANWEN

(Welsh and Manx.) Daughter of Llyr and sister to Bran. Consort to Matholwch, a King of Ireland.

BRIGID

(Irish, Welsh and British.) Also known as Brid, Bridey or Brigit. Goddess of fertility, inspiration and poetry. Daughter of the Dagda. Sometimes referred to as a triple Goddess (the three Brigids – maiden, mother and crone). Particularly associated with Spring and the festival of Imbolg. Christianised as St Bridget. Possibly a title or rank within the Priestess-hood of Avalon (Glastonbury) where there are archeological remains near the Tor called Bride's Mound.

CERRIDWEN

(Welsh.) Mother, Moon and Grain Goddess. She had a magic cauldron (called 'Amen') in which she made a magic potion called 'greal' which gave inspiration, wisdom and knowledge. The potion was made for her ugly son Avagdu, but Gwion who was given the task of stirring the potion accidentally sucked three drops from his finger and gained the wisdom. This resulted in a long chase by Cerridwen, allegorical for an initiation process, at the end of which Gwion was swallowed (as a grain of corn) and was then reborn as the bard Taliesin. Cerridwen is often depicted as the Dark Mother, and sometimes as consort to Cernnunos.

CORDELIA

(Welsh.) Maiden Goddess. Goddess of Truth and Knowledge. Daughter of Llyr.

DANA

(Irish – became synonymous with the Roman Diana.) A derivative of the Great Goddess Ana. More commonly associated with the full moon mother goddess aspect. Also associated with water, prosperity and wisdom.

DON
(Welsh.) Welsh equivalent of Dana or Ana. Queen of the Heavens, Goddess of sea and air. Consort of Bel. Mother of Arianrhod.

EPONA
(British and Gaulish.) Mother Goddess and Goddess of horses.

ERIN
(Irish.) A queen of the Tuatha de Danaan and daughter of the Dagda.

GODA
(British.) Otherwise known as Godiva. Spring love goddess associated with Beltane.

FLIDAIS
(Irish.) Goddess of woods and forests. Ruler of wild beasts.

MACHA
(Irish.) War Goddess, associated with Ulster. Mother goddess associated with the triple aspects of the Morrigan.

MARGAWSE
(Welsh.) Mother aspect of the triple goddess.

MODRON
(Welsh.) Great Mother goddess.

MORRIGAN
(Irish.) Morrigan is sometimes portrayed as a triple aspect but is also known as Morgana. Early Celtic moon goddess later associated with war and destruction. Associated with ravens. Also known as a dark temptress who devours her victims. Personified in the Arthurian myths as Arthur's half-sister.

OLWEN
(Welsh.) Fertility goddess associated with Beltane.

RHIANNON
(Welsh.) Fertility and otherworld goddess associated with the white horse. Many associations including the moon.

SCATHA
(Irish.) Dark goddess of the shadows. Underworld goddess with Scottish associations and with prophecy, magic, healing and blacksmiths.

CELTIC GODS

AENGUS
(Irish.) Also known as Angus or Aengus Mac Og (Mac Og means 'Son of the Virgin'). Young Love god, son of the Dagda.

BEL/GUL
(British.) Also known as Belinos or Belenos. Sun God. Originally Sumerian.

BRAN
(Manx and Welsh.) Also known as Bran the Blessed. A warrior god and brother of Branwen. Originally an Irish King who set off with an army of British to successfully avenge Ireland though he was mortally wounded. His head is said to have been buried in London, facing the English Channel in order to ward off invasions.

CERNUNNOS
The Celtic Horned God of nature. Most likely the same as other horned gods of other pagan paths and the Green Man.

COL
(Cornish – also Collan.) A Cornish derivative of Gul and Bel. Sometimes confused with St Collen a Glastonbury monk who is credited with banishing Gwynn Ap Nudd to the Underworld beneath Glastonbury Tor for all time and thus banishing the pagan deity from the area. Gwynn's entrapment is symbolised by the vesica sealed with a sword found around Glastonbury, especially at its Chalice Well Gardens.

THE DAGDA
(Irish.) The Good God – principal god of the Tuatha de Danaan.

DIANCECHT
(Irish.) Healer God of the Tuatha de Danaan.

DYLAN
(Welsh.) Sea God. Son of Arianrhod and Gwydion. Consort to the 'Lady of the Lake'.

GOIBNIU
(Irish.) Smith God or the Tuatha de Danaan. King of the gnomes.

GREEN MAN
(Common.) God of Nature.

GWYDION
(Welsh.) Brother of Arianrhod. Father of Lleu Llaw Gyffes with Arianrhod. Bardic God and musician. King of the British Celts.

GWYNN
(Welsh.) Also known as Gwynn ap Nudd. God of the Underworld and leader of the Wild Hunt. Similar correspondences to Herne.

GWYTHYR

HERNE
(British.) See Gwynn.

HORNED ONE
See Green Man. The figure of a horned god is common to the history of most early pagan religions.

LLEU LLAW GYFFES
(Welsh.) Celtic God of Youth. Son of Arianrhod and Gwydion. Welsh equivalent of Lugh.

LLYR
(Welsh, Irish and Manx.) Also known as Lir. Father of Creiddylad (or Cordelia a maiden goddess), Branwen and Bran. Also known as a King of the Tuatha de Danaan under which guise he was a consort first to Aebh from which a daughter and three sons were born (Fionuala, Hugh, Fiacha and Conn). After Aebh died he married Aoife who turned the four children into swans out of jealousy. Corresponds to Shakespeare's King Lear.

LUGH
(Irish.) Sun God. Also God of many arts. Commanded the forces of the Tuatha de Danaan against Formorian invaders.

MANANNAN MAC LIR
(Irish and Manx.) Sea God. His name is given to the Isle of Man.

MATH MATHONWY
(Welsh.) A god of magic. He taught his craft to his nephew Gwydion.

MERLIN
(Welsh and British.) Also known as Myrddin or Emrys. Early bard, magician and seer, later associated with the Arthurian legends. Merlin possibly became a title or rank of high order within the Druidic tradition.

NUDD
(British.) Also known as Ludd, Llud or Nuda. River God. Lends his name to Ludgate in London.

OGMA
(Irish.) God of writing and wisdom. Also known as a warrior god of the Tuatha de Danaan. Mythic inventor of the Ogham runic script.

PWYLL
(Welsh.) King of Annwn, God of the Otherworld. First consort to Rhiannon.

TALIESIN
(Welsh.) A bardic fertility god. Son of Cerridwen who gave birth to him after swallowing Gwion in a bardic initiation myth.

TANNUS
(British.) Thunder god.

NAMES GIVEN TO THE LUNAR MONTHS

The names given to the months of the moon throughout the year vary considerably even through the Celtic pathway. These are those that I have settled on using as they feel right to me . . .

January – Wolf Moon
February – Storm Moon
March – Chaste Moon
April – Seed Moon
May – Hare Moon
June – Dyad Moon
July – Mead Moon
August – Corn Moon
September – Harvest Moon

October – Blood Moon
November – Snow Moon
December – Cold Moon

There are generally thirteen Full Moons in a solar year. The thirteenth moon is given the name of Blue Moon and is the second full moon that occurs within a calendar month.

COLOUR CORRESPONDENCES

The following colour correspondences can be used to help add weight to a candle spell.

BLACK	Negativity, malice, death, night. North.
BLUE (Dark)	Water, healing, third eye chakra.
BLUE (Light)	Air, throat chakra.
BROWN	Earth.
GOLD	The Sun God, health, wealth and harmony.
GREEN	The Goddess. Venus. Love and compassion. Heat chakra.
GREY	Evening. West.
ORANGE	Solar plexus chakra.
PINK	Love, desire.
PURPLE	Healing, passion. Crown chakra.
RED	The God. Mars, fire, courage, passion. Base chakra.
SILVER	The Goddess. The Moon.
WHITE	Purity, South, magic – the power of light.
YELLOW	Air, clear thought, harmony. Spleen chakra.

ELEMENTAL TABLE OF CORRESPONDENCES

	Earth	Air	Fire	Water
Symbol	▽ (earth glyph)	△ (air glyph)	△	▽
Direction	North	East	South	West
Astrological signs	Taurus, Virgo and Capricorn	Aquarius, Gemini and Libra	Leo, Aries and Sagittarius	Scorpio, Pisces and Cancer
Colour	Black or Green	Red or Yellow	White or Red	Grey or Blue
Elemental form	Gnome	Sylph or fairy	Salamander	Ondine
Season	Winter	Spring	Summer	Autumn
Goddesses	Cerridwen	Brigid or Rhiannon	Morgana or Macha	Arianrhod
Gods	Cernnunos	Ogma or Dagda	Lugh, Bran or Bel	Llyr
Time of day	Night	Dawn	Noon	Sunset
Power	Wisdom	Enlightenment	Future or destiny	Balance
Movement	Down	In	Out	Up
Organ	Kidneys	Lungs	Liver	Heart
Positive emotion	Safety	Discernment	Motivation	Love and joy
Negative emotion	Fear	Judgement	Anger	Depression
Human function	Physical	Psychosomatic	Energy	Biochemistry
Daily life	Work	Social	Self	Home
Mental power	Sensation	Thought	Intuition	Feelings
Complementary treatment for weakness	Massage, physiotherapy, osteopathy	Counselling and aromatherapy	Acupuncture and energy healing	Nutrition and herbal

ELEMENTAL TABLE OF CORRESPONDENCES – *continued*

	Earth	Air	Fire	Water
Symbol	▽ (with bar)	△ (with bar)	△	▽
Represented by	Salt	Incense	Candles	Water
Herbs	Alfalfa; barley; blackthorn; buckwheat; clover; fumitort; honeysuckle; patchouli; pine; elm; primrose; rhubarb; soapwort; sorrel; sage; strawberry; tansy; vervain;	Agrimony; almond; benzoin; bergamot; caraway; cedar; chicory; comfrey; dandelion; dill; dock; elecampne; fenugreek; fern; hazel; hop; lavender; lemon verbena; marjoram; mint; mistletoe; nutmeg; parsley; sandalwood	Alder; basil; bay; betony; celandine; cinnamon; cinqfoil; clove; coriander; dragon's blood; garlic; gorse; juniper; mandrake; mustard; nettle; oak; olive; rosemary; saffron; st john's wort; sunflower	Aloe vera; apple; ash; balm gilead; belladonna; birch; bindweed; burdock; camphor; catnip; coltsfoot; cornflower; daisy; dog rose; feverfew; foxglove; hemp; herb robert; iris; ivy; jasmine; lady's mantle; lily; mugwort; myrrh; rose; rowan; poppy; scilcap; thyme; valerian; violet; willow; woad; yarrow; yew
Crystals and minerals	Agate (green and moss); aventurine; coal; emerald; jasper; jet; malachite; marble; obsidian; onyx; peridot; quartz (smoky); salt; tourmaline (black)	Amethyst; citrine; emerald; flourite; jade; jasper (mottled); lapis lazuli; moonstone, topaz (yellow) and turquoise	Agate (red); amber; bloodstone; carnelian; diamond; garnet; haematite; iron; jasper (red); ruby; sulphur; tiger's eye.	Agate (blue lace); amethyst; aquamarine; coral; jade; lapis lazuli; moonstone; mother of pearl; pearl; sapphire; silver; sodalite; sugalite
Tarot suit	Pentacles	Swords	Wands	Cups
Chakra correspondence	Base	Heart	Solar Plexus	Spleen
Tool	Pentacle	Athame or sword	Wand	Chalice

21

BIBLIOGRAPHY

Doreen Valiente	An ABC of Witchcraft	Hale	1973
Dion Fortune	Applied Magic	Aquarian	1962
Gerald Gardner	Book of Shadows (3 versions)	(unpublished)	1949
Ross Nicholls	Book of Druidry, The	Thorsons	1990
Shalila Sharamon	Chakra Handbook, The	Lotus Light	1991
Raymond Buckland	Complete Book of Witchcraft	Llewellyn	1997
Riane Eisler	Chalice and the Blade, The	Thorsons	1987
RJ Stewart	Celtic Gods, Celtic Goddesses	Blandford	1990
DJ Conway	Celtic Magic	Llewellyn	1998
Caitlin Matthews	Celtic Tradition, The	Element	1989
Andy Baggott	Celtic Wisdom	Piatkus	1999
Scott Cunningham	Crystal, Gem and Metal Magic	Llewellyn	1997
Marion Weinstein	Earth Magic	Earth Magic	1998
Amber Wolfe	Elemental Power	Llewellyn	1996
TFG Dexter	Fire Worship	Oak Magic	1998
Aleister Crowley	Gems from the Equinox	New Falcon	1974
Israel Regardie	Golden Dawn, The	Llewellyn	1998
John Matthews	Healing the Wounded King	Earth Quest	1997
S Lavendar & A Franklin	Herb Craft	Capall Bann	1996
T Freke & P Gandy	Jesus Mysteries, The	Thorsons	1999
Jeffrey Gantz (trans)	Mabinogion, The	Penguin Classics	1976
Dion Fortune	Machinery of the Mind	Society of Inner Light	1995
D Jason Cooper	Mithras, Mysteries & Initiation	Weiser	1996
Julian Cope	Modern Antiquarian, The	Thorsons	1998
Dion Fortune	Mystical Qabala, The	Society of Inner Light	1935
J D Wakefield	Legendary Landscapes	Nod Press	1999
Gwynn	Light from the Shadows	Capall Bann	1999
Z F Lansdowne	Rays and Esoteric Psychology, The	Weiser	1989
Pauline Campanelli	Rites of Passage	Llewellyn	1994
Raven Grimassi	Wiccan Mysteries, The	Llewellyn	1997
Scott Cunningham	Living Wicca	Llewellyn	1997
Laurie Cabot	Power of the Witch	Penguin Arkana	1990
Nancy B Watson	Practical Solitary Magic	Weiser	1996
Eliphas Levi	Transcendental Magic (translation)	Senate	1995
David Goddard	Tower of Alchemy, The	Weiser	1999
Rhianon Ryall	West Country Wicca	Capall Bann	1993
Caitlin & John Matthews	Western Way, The	Penguin Arkana	1985
Robert Graves	White Goddess, The	Faber and Faber	1948
John Phillip Rhodes	Wicca Unveiled	Speaking Tree	1999
Janet & Stuart Farrar	Witches Bible, A	Phoenix	1996
Ronald Hutton	Triumph of the Moon, The	Oxford	2001
Vivianne Crowley	Wicca	Thorsons	1996